GOING THROUGH
THE JOURNEY OF HEALING

SHARON GOTTFRIED LEWIS

WHAT PEOPLE ARE SAYING ABOUT...

I love Pastor Sharon Lewis's passion for healing. Do you need healing? This book will strengthen your faith. As you read this book prayerfully, the Holy Spirit will whisper to your heart, "Healing is *yours*!"

Bob Sorge, author, *God's Still Writing Your Story*

Sharon Lewis has captured the Heart of God in "Going Through"! She skillfully shows us numerous steps that we must take as the Lord leads us from captivity to liberty. Her combination of scriptural teaching and testimonies of healings make the book an appealing journey for the reader. I have personally witnessed the Lord use Sharon over and over in walking people through to glorious healings! "Going Through" is a treasure chest of revelation and inspiration!

Rev. Janet Shell, Worship Leader, Founder Worship to the Nations
www.worshiptothenations.com

What Rev. Dr. Sharon Lewis has captured in the pages of GOING THROUGH: *A Journey of Healing* resonates profoundly with the life-changing journey I and my family have experienced for the last 25 years. Scripture, theological understanding, inner healing concepts, and real life experiences are beautifully woven together across the pages of this book. The reader is challenged to deeply engage first with God, then with self, and finally with others for fullness of truth and godly empowerment which are found when Divine Healing touches body, soul, and spirit.

Geralynn Gardner, Compelled By Grace, Inc., author, *"Hearts That Matter Much: Bringing Children to the Healing Love of Jesus"*

Dr. Lewis skillfully weaves together biblical reflection, academic analysis, personal testimony, and the wisdom of over twenty-five years of pastoral ministry to create a comprehensive and practical introduction to the journey of healing. This book will equip pastors and congregational leaders to begin laying the foundation for ministries of healing in their own contexts. In an age when members of our churches are searching for deeper emotional and spiritual freedom, Dr. Lewis offers a timely word of hope and encouragement that true and lasting healing can be found in Jesus Christ.

The Rev. Dr. Douglas F. Scharf ~ Rector, Good Shepherd of Episcopal Church and School in Tequesta, Florida.

I have known Pastor Sharon Lewis for close to a decade and a half. In that time I have seen her grow from pastor and teacher to scholar and author. Her newest book, "Going Through" is both content comprehensive and spiritually challenging. It shows her pastoral sensitivity and her scholarly capacity. "Going Through" is an Illustrative book filled with both personal and the stories of others that reveal deep theological impressions. The book is also Informational as it shares important research consultations, teachers, and authors. Sharons writing is deeply Instructional as it comprehensively reveals scriptural background and further theological evidence. Finally, "Going Through" is inspirational in that it is both God Breathed and gives personal Holy Spiritual strength and empowerment to the Saints in the Church where God is our Doctor and Jesus is our Physician.

I'm pleased to recommend Dr. Lewis' newest book to readers hungry for spiritual strength. Sharon is a priest with a consistent attribute. She is filled with spiritual joy that she shares with loving encouragement. Her joy comes through in all of these pages!

The Rt. Rev. Dabney T. Smith, Bishop, The Episcopal Diocese of Southwest Florida

Dr. Sharon Lewis has given us an opportunity to learn the depths of healing in a practical and personal way. It is a book which comes out of her own experience. There is a sense of victory filling the pages and inspiring the reader to risk, trust, and pray.

The Rev. Joseph K Acton, North American Director, OSL; Author of *A Powerful Joy* and *Night Light.*

Finally! A book on healing that reminds us that just a little, or even no faith at all, is enough. The Rev. Dr. Sharon Lewis has led workshops and seminars on healing for decades. This book is the culmination of her years in the healing ministry. Through biblical stories and the many personal stories of healing journeys, you will learn that 'healing is the very heart of God.' And here's the best part; you will learn how God heals, why God wants you to heal and how to grow closer to him. Frankly, I love this book not just because it is written well and is an easy read, but for all the practical and spiritual messages within.

The Reverend Danielle Morris ~ co-author of *30 Days Towards Healing Your Grief,* and founder of Walking the Mourners Path.

Copyright © 2019 by Sharon Lynn Gottfried Lewis

Going Through: A Journey in Inner Healing
By Sharon Lynn Gottfried Lewis

Printed in the United States of America.
ISBN: 978-1-7334709-0-2

All rights reserved solely by the author. The author guarantees all contents are original and do not infringe upon the legal rights of any other person or work. No part of this book may be reproduced in any form without the permission of the author. The views expressed in this book are not necessarily those of the publisher.

Unless otherwise noted, Scripture quotations are taken from THE HOLY BIBLE, NEW INTERNATIONAL VERSION®, NIV® Copyright © 1973, 1978, 1984, 2011 by Biblica, Inc.® Used by permission. All rights reserved worldwide.

Scripture quotations marked nasb are taken from the New American Standard Bible®. ©1960, 1962, 1963, 1968, 1971, 1972, 1973, 1975, 1977, 1995 by The Lockman Foundation. Used by permission. (www.Lockman.org)

Scripture quotations marked KJV are taken from the King James Version of the Bible.

Scripture quotations marked ESV are taken from the English Standard Version copyright ©2001 by Crossway, a publishing ministry of Good News Publishers. ESV® text has been reproduced in cooperation with and by permission of Good News Publishers. Used by permission. All rights reserved.

DEDICATION

This book is dedicated to my precious family whom I love more than I can even express, Brian, Kristy and Zoe Lewis and dear friends on the healing journey and the thousands of people who yearn for freedom and healing through Jesus Christ. The Lord has need of you! Let the healing begin…

ACKNOWLEDGEMENT

I have so many people to thank for the publication of this book, too numerous to mention here. I am so grateful to the many friends and family members who speak into my life and walk with me on my healing journey. Also the blessing of being allowed to walk with so many others on their healing journeys is humbling. I would be remiss if I did not mention a few of you who have painstakingly helped with editing and other details in this project. Thank you from the bottom of my heart MaryAnne Moran, Lora Reed and the Fiverr team. Thanks for the encouragement I've received from the people who wrote recommendations for this book: Bishop Dabney Smith, Rev Janet Shell, Bob Sorge, Geralyn Gardner, Rev Dr Doug Scharf, Rev Danielle Morris, and Rev Josh Acton. Others who played a role in spiritually lifting me up throughout the process of writing this book are Kathy Bennett, Rev Robin Morical, the Lilys, and Amazing Love Healing Ministry Board members. Thank you for investing in my life and for being available to pray and just talk. Thank you to all who continue to journey with me in this amazing healing ministry. Together we are better. God has need of all of us.

Most of all I give thanks to Jesus Christ, my Lord. my Savior and my Healer. Even when I thought about not finishing this book, You never left me Lord. Even through physical challenges and tight schedules, You just waited and once again lifted me up, raising me up to complete the work You had commissioned me to write four years ago. You are so faithful and loving. Thank You. I am one whom You have healed and continue healing for Your glory and the journey continues....

TABLE OF CONTENTS

What people are saying about … 2

Dedication 6

Acknowledgement i

Introduction 1

Chapter 1 | Does God Heal?... 5

Chapter 2 | What is Inner Healing?...31

Chapter 3 | Healing Unhealed Hurts and Unmet Needs.............................47

Chapter 4 | Blocks to Healing: *Identity Issues Slumbering Spirit* 61

Chapter 5 | Blocks to Healing: *Inner Vows, Word Curses, Lies of the Enemy, Generational Sin* 95

Chapter 6 | Forgiveness 121

Chapter 7 | Spiritual Authority And Warfare 139

Chapter 8 | Where's The Power? 161

Chapter 9 | Walking Out Your Healing In Daily Victory 179

Works Consulted... 186

Contact Information: 192

INTRODUCTION

The title for this book came through a stranger. At the end of an Amazing Love Healing Conference at a church in the Orlando, Florida area, with food in hand, I found a quiet place in a room off from the main dining area. Lowering my tired, but contented body down in the comfortable chair, I began reflecting on the wonderful healing work God had done this weekend. He used our entire team to reach these precious people. What a love-healing movement of God! Several people stopped in to share their witnesses of how God had healed deep wounds within them. One man in particular stopped in with his son. Alex was a large man who suffered with several serious medical disabilities.

"I didn't think God could heal me. I fought this whole thing," he said, his voice choking with emotion. That was not a revelation; I had seen the resistance in his body language throughout the conference. You know what I mean, arms folded, stern look on his face, just daring God to do something.

"He healed me! I'm free of the anger and the rejection! It's gone!" His face was beaming. "And I want the Holy Spirit." He had not come forward toward the end of the conference for prayer for the baptism of the Holy Spirit. So right there we prayed and God's Holy Spirit filled him.

After Alex and his son left, a gentleman walked in, sat down next to me and said matter-of-factly, "I know the title of your book." *What?* I hadn't even mentioned that I was writing a book on healing. "You do?" I queried, eyes wide open. "Yes, it's going to be called *Going Through*." It hit me like a ton of bricks! Yes, that is the title of this book God has given me to write. Amazing how God sends you who you need at just the right time if you're open to Him.

"How did you come upon that title?" I asked him. And he smiled as he began to explain. At one point in the conference one of our anointed women from the ministry danced. The music and the dance were choreographed to help people give those blocked areas in need of healing to Jesus: rage, depression, ungodly sorrow, addiction, unmet needs and other issues. About fifteen seconds into the dance the music stopped. The dancer backing up, signalled the sound man to try again. Again after fifteen seconds the music stopped. Immediately our worship leader sat down at the keyboard and began to play prophetically. The dancer danced! The piano player and the dancer were one as she began to pull out labels from the garbage bag. Each one represented that place in our souls that stores negative events. And wounds from the past. Weeping could be heard throughout the room as people found the courage to give these wounds to God. One man jumped up as the dancer came down the aisle with the label rage in her hands exclaiming "That's mine!" With tears in his eyes he released pent up rage that had been building for many years. "I've just gone through a healing in my small group and now this finishes it," he said as he grabbed that label and tore it in two. His wife wept with tears of joy and relief.

My prophetic friend who knew the name of my book explained, "What I was watching was *Going Through*. When the music stopped the dancer passed through the difficulty of the music stopping and starting. She passed through the challenge. When the labels representing the blocked places were displayed, people were able to go through with healing. It was obvious they went through in the name of Jesus Christ.

Curious I asked my new friend his occupation: "I'm an editor." God is so interesting!

So *Going Through* it is. *Going Through* is about going through life with all its joys and sorrows, storms and peaceful times, wilderness voids and valleys with God. It is about the journey of healing and the process of reconciliation and forgiveness covered with God's love. We really do go through life in and with our Lord Jesus Christ.

The journey of healing is all about going through life with God. His agape love is kneaded into our souls transforming us, enabling us to give to others all that He's given us.

> *I have no silver and gold, but what I do have I give to you.*
> **(Acts 3:6 KJV)**

In conclusion, St Augustine wrote: "The words printed here are concepts. You must go through the experiences." (Internet cited Brainy Quote, "St Augustine quotes", accessed December 3, 2016). That is my prayer for each one of you as you read this book. May you read, inwardly digest and experience even more of God's deep, transforming love and healing grace.

Chapter 1
DOES GOD HEAL?

Newly ordained to the Episcopal priesthood I attended one of Rita Bennet's *Emotionally Free* conferences. Sitting on the front row, not wanting to miss a thing, I heard Rita ask: "Who *do you feel* first loved you?" Not who should have but who do you feel first loved you? Stunned by the question, I searched and searched. Fear in the form of a lump rose up in my throat. I couldn't name anyone! Tears began to well up inside but I held them in unsure of what was going on in me. Later, I asked Rita if she would pray with me. At the end of the day she brought me into a quiet prayer room.

"What is it?" she gently asked.

The lump in my throat was still there as my tears spilled over. *I couldn't think of anyone who I could honestly say was the first one who really loved me.*

She prayed prayers of protection over both of us, She asked in the name of Jesus Christ for the Holy Spirit to guide us and lead us to the root of this fear of not being loved and the deep heartache I felt inside.

Suddenly, I see myself as a baby about six months old, with a shock of red hair, bright green eyes and chunky legs going a mile a minute. I could see this picture in my mind's eye as I was cradled in these magnificent, strong arms. I knew whose arms they were. Jesus Himself was holding me! My face was radiant and filled with joy. Who wouldn't be, resting in the arms of Jesus? Then I saw a man standing in the distance with his head down. He was about the length of a long church aisle away. My joyful mood changed. I knew who he was even though I had never seen a picture of him. He was my biological father - the man who left my mother, my three and a half year old brother and me. I had barely been on this earth when he left us to fend for ourselves.

I was stunned to see him, but even more stunning and was what I heard Jesus saying, *Come closer to this man and let him hold you.*

Everything inside of me rose up in anger and resistance: "No!" I yelled. Ha! I discovered that babies have that 'no' inside long before they turn two!

Closer and closer we came to where this man was standing. I knew it was Jesus moving, not me. I couldn't even crawl yet. I saw a short cigar, known as a stogie, sticking out of his mouth. His head was still down and he was very sad. Yet the resistance in me remained. Before I could blink I was right next to him though still in Jesus' arms. I saw the tear coming down his left cheek and instantly a *yes* rose up in me as Jesus transferred me into this man's arms. I do know him. I had never met him but I know him. He was my biological father. The one who walked away from us. I didn't find out that my step-father, whom I adored, was not my biological father until I was in seventh grade. I didn't even know what my biological father looked like but now Jesus had shown me.

As I lay in my biological father's arms, staring at him I noticed his tears trickling down his cheeks. He softly said: "It was never about you."

What?! My inner child so needed to hear that! I cried and I cried. Buckets and buckets of tears poured out from somewhere deep inside. You see for years I held onto self-blame and guilt. I thought I had caused my parents' divorce. After all, I was one more mouth to feed when they had very little money. The family story I overheard once was that he tried to talk my mother into aborting me, but she resisted. Yet here he was saying it wasn't about me! My heart grew lighter as I forgave him from the little six-month-old's heart. Mentally, as an adult, I had certainly forgiven him but true heart forgiveness has to come from the one who was so deeply wounded, so abandoned and rejected and that was the little one living inside me. *The truth will set you free,* (John 8:31, ESV) became a living reality in my life.

Does God heal? Yes! He most certainly does!

Sometimes doubts arise, however because a person has prayed for a sick person who has not recovered. Sometimes it is asked because people are unsure about who God is in their lives. The Old Testament scripture answers this question by affirming the following:

I Am the God who heals you…

> *If you will diligently listen to the voice of the Lord your God, and do that which is right in his eyes, and give ear to his commandments and keep all his statutes, I will put none of the diseases on you that I put on the Egyptians, for I am the Lord, your healer*
> **(Exodus 15.26 ESV)**.

> *He heals the brokenhearted and binds up their wounds.*
> **(Psalm 147:3 ESV)**.

He is the God who heals us.

New Testament Scripture demonstrates the veracity of that statement:

> *And Jesus went throughout all the cities and villages, teaching in their synagogues and proclaiming the gospel of the kingdom and healing every disease and every affliction.*
> **(Matthew 9:35 ESV)**

> *God anointed Jesus of Nazareth with the Holy Spirit and with power. He went about doing good and healing all who were oppressed by the devil, for God was with him*
> **(Acts 10:38 ESV)**

Jesus is the pathway to healing and redemption. His own death and resurrection is healing and reconciliation for God and His people. The cross is the fulfillment of God the healer.

Healing: The Character of God

Healing as proclaimed by God is who He is and what He does, demonstrated through His Son, Jesus Christ. He is about healing of whole person - spirit, soul, and body.

> *And he went throughout all Galilee, teaching in their synagogues and proclaiming the gospel of the kingdom and healing every disease and every affliction among the people*
> **(Mathew 4:23 ESV)**.

The Greek and Hebrew words for healing provide an in-depth understanding of what healing means. The Greek word for healing, θεραπεύω (*therapeuō*), used in this scripture, means to serve, do service, to heal, cure, restore to health and to worship. There is a reference in the Greek definition of this word to the wounding in a person which impedes or even prevents him from being of service to God or even worshipping freely. This wounding can be physical, mental, emotional, psychological, social, and spiritual – some are a combination of more than one. The definition of healing in the Greek encompasses a full multi-level understanding of healing. Another Greek word for healing, ἰάομαι (*iaomai*), used in Acts 4.30, means to cure, make whole, be free from sin and error, and bring about one's salvation as a witness of wholeness. The emphasis on healing here is understood ultimately as salvation, (1 Peter 2:24 ESV; James 5:16 ESV). The Greek word, σῴζω, (*sozo*) is usually translated *save* as in Matthew 1.21, *He will save his people from their sins*. It can also carry the meaning of *cure*. In Luke 8:36, the demon-possessed man was *cured* or *saved*. Both the Greek and the Hebrew definitions for healing give us a more complete picture of God's healing. It encompasses everything in us, spirit, soul and body.

How does healing fit into the whole God story, including His plan, His vision, His mission, and his character? The Hebrew word for heal is *rapha*, to be cured, repaired, restored, and made whole from hurts, defects and distresses. The word restored is defined as returning, bringing back, refreshing, and reversing. Within God's healing is restoration. One name for God is Jehovah Rapha: God the Healer. It is His character, His DNA to heal. It is who He is. The Hebrew name for doctor is *rofe*. We could be bold and say God is our Doctor! Jesus is our Physician!

God's purpose for us as individuals is to be healed in order to be transformed and conformed into the image of His Son, Jesus Christ.

> *For those God foreknew he also predestined to be conformed to the likeness of his Son that he might be the firstborn among many brothers.*
> **(Rom. 8:29 NIV).**

The more we are healed the more able we are to love God and others with God's unconditional love. Peter's reinstatement by the resurrected Jesus is not a return to what he was before but an invitation to become more, brand new and live as transformative love; the very character of God Himself on this earth (John 21). This is where the healing begins for all of us. Jesus saves us. Jesus befriends us. And eventually we grow into a sacrificial love of Jesus and His people.

Healing is not only for the individual but for the corporate people of God. Corporate healing is implied in both the books of Leviticus and 2 Chronicles. Leviticus uses the reconditioning of a house that had been contaminated with mildew as an example of the cleansing nature of healing, *'pronounce the house clean, for the disease is healed'* (Leviticus14.48; Monroe & Schwab, 2009, p 123). Monroe and Schwab assert that in 2 Chronicles 7:14 the Israelites are corporately considered as one body suffering from a wound and in need of healing, When one hurts, all hurt. When one is blessed we all are blessed. We are connected through the blood of Jesus Christ. We are kin!

> *If my people who are called by my name humble themselves, pray, and seek my face, and turn from their wicked ways, then I will hear from heaven, and I will forgive their sin and heal their land (2009, 123).*

Churches need healing; not just individuals.

The small congregation was gathered waiting for my team and I to arrive. This was a big step for them, asking for help. A year ago their church had split over divisive issues in the denomination. A small rag tag, discouraged. beat up group was left to maintain this church. Walking into this old church we immediately sensed the discouragement and loss of hope. Their faces were sad. We sang a few worship songs but their hearts weren't in it. My team kept quietly interceding for the Holy Spirit to move.

I asked them: "Does God heal?" Stunned at first by the question they began to respond:

"Where was God when our church split?"

"We lost best friends."

"We don't even speak to some of them anymore and our kids were baptized together."

"How could God let this happen?"

The pain was etched on their faces and could be heard in their muted voices. Together we looked back at the history of this church. Some of the matriarchs and patriarchs of the church reminded them of the initial vision: To come to know Christ and live in Christian community. We began praying praying the I AM scriptures over them (found at the end of Chapter Two) both corporately and individually. God began the healing of deep wounds through His spoken word.

Later in the day we explored words that had been spoken against the church and each other and wounds that had never been healed from past history. They weren't hiding anymore. We prayed healing prayers in small groups and in large group ministry time, we watched God dismantle the defensive walls they had erected in response to this church split. We ended the day with forgiveness. They spoke out forgiveness to those who had left and then forgiveness to one another. As they hugged each other with some weeping the healing had indeed begun. The Bible uses the word countenance, which means the appearance on the face. They no longer looked downcast, genuine smiles had replaced the downtrodden frowns. The love of God showed on their faces. The original vision was not lost but had certainly gone through testing and now they were coming through this time of brokenness to become stronger than before. That is the journey of healing.

Role of God as Healer

In Allan Coppedge's (2009) *Portraits of God: A Biblical Theology of Holiness*, his thesis is based on the fact that God wants to be known by us and in that process of knowing Him, God would become the most important One and the most important relationship in our life. He becomes our very purpose for living (11). God reveals Himself to us in a variety of roles or portraits throughout Scripture. Coppedge (2009) sees the identification and examination of these roles as possible doors that will allow us to know God better and in deeper ways. The roles he identifies are the following: Creator, King, Personal Revealer, Priest, Judge, Father, Redeemer, and Shepherd. He has chosen the attribute of holiness which connects both Old and New testaments, and unifies the roles of God, as well as the basic doctrinal themes of salvation, creation, humanity, sin and healing. God's holiness permeates everything because God is holy. God can be seen as Healer through the various, yet integrated roles of God fills.

God the Creator as Healer

We have discovered that an obstacle to healing may be rooted in the conflict of how people think God sees them, what He intends for them to be, and their human, sinful behavior especially towards themselves. As Coppedge notes: "Humanness and sinfulness are not to be viewed as identical" (2009, p. 374). The negative effects on an individual who has been harmed or the harm someone has done to others is not who God created that person to be. Our identity is rooted in being a child of God, created by Him in His image.

For you formed my inward parts; you knitted me together in my mother's womb

(Psalm 139:13).

To knit together in Hebrew means not only to be interwoven with God's image and constructed by Him, but to be covered over and protected by Him, like a hedge is made to guard and protect a garden.

Our identity as a child of God can be marred by hurts inflicted on us, especially as a young child, or when basic needs are not being met, especially by parents. During these hurtful times the Creator is not seen as a good God or a good Parent. This conflict between the images of the Heavenly Father with one's earthly father is devastating especially when sexual abuse has happened in a family. It is hard to remember you are chosen by God for all the right reasons and yet chosen by your earthly father for all the wrong reasons. Parents can inflict emotional wounds on their children by harsh discipline, abandonment, neglect, and even simply not listening or ignoring them.

The Israelites knew that they were God's chosen people.

For you are a people holy to the Lord your God, and the Lord has chosen you to be a people for his treasured possession, out of all the peoples who are on the face of the earth

(Deut. 14:2).

Behold, please look, we are all your people

(Isa. 64:9b; Ps.95:7).

Yet, the Israelites even after being delivered from the Egyptians, and being cared for by God in the wilderness, wanted to run back to their old way of living. Their enemy's wilderness which is slavery and death looked more inviting than facing the challenges of God's wilderness which is obedience, belief, and freedom.

God's people were ready to step into the Promised Land. They sent out twelve, a reconnaissance team, to spy on the inhabitants of Cana, the Promised Land, Ten of them come back with a very discouraging report of the fierce people who live there. The spirit of discouragement sets in, bringing them back to their identity as slaves rather than a free people chosen by God.

> *Why is the LORD bringing us into this land, to fall by the sword? Our wives and our little ones will become a prey. Would it not be better for us to go back to Egypt?*
>
> (Num.14:3).

Discouragement, if not attended to, will bring unbelief and rebellion. The Israelites gave credit to the word of the spies rather than the word of God. When we are hurt or angry and full of rage, we too can display dysfunctional behaviors. Like those of the ancient Israelites, our behaviors demonstrate the deep wounding that lies beneath. When we allow ourselves to live in negative patterns, we live as slaves to our wounds rather than children of Almighty God.

God the Father as Healer

The young single mom sitting in front of me looked worn out with work, children and relationships. And she was worn out with herself. Eyes cast down she softly admitted: "I don't pick good men." The tears began to flow as she talked about her childhood. Her father was violent!

He would drink and become abusive especially to their mother. Her older brother was trained to quickly grab her and run into the closet and hide when dad became violent. They could hear him hitting their mother. Her brother would tell her stories trying to keep her quiet and calm. After the noise died down, he would peek out to see if it was clear to come out. She spent a lot of time in that closet. I asked her if she would allow me to pray for her. Before I could say much, she said: "Jesus is here in the closet!" He was holding both her and her brother. Peace filled them both. Then Jesus opened the closet door and brought them out. She could see Jesus holding their mother. I asked "Where is your father?" "He's gone," she said, "He…he's gone! …he's just gone!" Standing together with their mom Jesus attended to their wounded hurts. I asked her if she was willing to forgive her father in that particular scene. She hesitated. This was hard. After a while she was willing to do that and she began to feel relief as she released her father of her judgement, and released him to Jesus.

She sat up straighter as she began to review her male relationships and she soon saw a pattern of picking emotionally abusive men and men who drank too much. In the name of Jesus Christ, she repented for her decisions and we broke these unhealthy patterns. We also broke the unhealthy image of her earthly father with her heavenly Father.

"I feel light!" she said. After sealing this healing in the name of the Father, Son and Holy Spirit and blessing her, we hugged and she almost skipped out the door.

Lack of intimacy is an area where many people need healing. Some people, who come for healing, have great difficulty relating to God the Father. Often that is related to sexual or physical abuse from a male. It is especially prominent when the abuse is from a relative, such as one's father. Lack of intimacy in men or women can also be the result of an absent father or mother physically or emotionally.

Attachment disorder at birth, where baby and mother did not have the opportunity to bond appropriately can cause intimacy issues later with God, parents, and other relationships.

God the Judge as Healer

Shall not the Judge of all the earth do what is just?
Gen. 18:25b

Abraham queries God concerning the city of Sodom (Gen.18:25b). Seeing God as a righteous judge starts with the understanding of God's role as lawmaker in the Garden of Eden. Here in the role of Judge through the person of a loving Father, God gives fatherly direction to Adam concerning the tree he was not to eat from (Gen. 2:16-17). God continues that role all through Scripture speaking directives, commands, and guidance in both written and oral forms. God does this for the good of His people. God is good in His very essence and will only operate from that standpoint. This brings a deeper and more loving view of healing when dealing with conviction of sin issues, disobedience, and rebelliousness. These issues can be part of one's negative behavioral patterns even while in the process of inner healing. With the image of God as Judge who is always our Father in that role, the disciplinary actions of God are softened and can even be embraced by the sinner because of this fuller knowledge of God. Problems with authority can stem from faulty understandings of God as Judge divorced from His role as Holy Father. He is healer in both roles.

Judith's Testimony

Judith came into my office obviously discouraged. The stooped shoulders and shuffling gait gave her away. Yet in her eyes anger was very present.

With her piercing eyes narrowed, she spoke: "I have been hurt too much by these people."

She was a pastor's wife and we had prayed several times over this same issue of feeling that the parishioners expected too much of her and were abusive to her. All for naught it seemed. Little had changed as confirmed in assessing her continued negative responses. This time I brought in a new prayer partner hoping for new direction from the Holy Spirit. Frankly I was tired too for the healing did not seem to last.

"Nothing is working," she stated as if reading my mind! As she rambled on in her discontent, finally she let out what was on her heart, "Well God just isn't healing me or the situation."

After having my prayer partner open up with a prayer of protection, I uttered deep within myself, *Help!* I waited for the Holy Spirit….and I waited it seemed interminably long until suddenly God brought to me the healing of Miriam in Scripture (Numbers 12: 1-16).

The story involves Aaron and Miriam, brother and sister of Moses, who spoke against Moses, the leader of the Israelites because of the Cushite woman whom he had married. Aaron, the mouthpiece for Moses, and Miriam, revered and honored prophetess, were in top leadership with Moses, the head leader as chosen by God. Prompted by God I began to tell the story as if it were happening right there in that room. And lo and behold, it did.

> *And Aaron and Miriam said, "Has the LORD indeed spoken only through Moses? Has he not spoken through us also?" And the LORD heard it.*
>
> *And suddenly the LORD said to Moses and to Aaron and Miriam, "Come out, you three, to the tent of meeting." And the three of them came out.*

And the LORD came down in a pillar of cloud and stood at the entrance of the tent and called Aaron and Miriam, and they both came forward.

Judith began to identify with Miriam and perhaps what she was thinking. Whew! I'm here in the presence of God...He is calling me forward. I'm trembling, yet excited. Surely God has heard my complaint...my plea for a change. After all God does speak through me.

And God said, 'Hear my words: If there is a prophet among you, I the LORD make myself known to him in a vision; I speak with him in a dream. Not so with my servant Moses. He is faithful in all my house. With him I speak mouth to mouth, clearly, and not in riddles, and he beholds the form of the LORD. Why then were you not afraid to speak against my servant Moses?'

And the anger of the LORD was kindled against them, and he departed.

When the cloud removed from over the tent, behold, Miriam was leprous, like snow. And Aaron turned toward Miriam, and behold, she was leprous.

Continuing on with the story: Suddenly Miriam's skin was mottled with white blemishes...deadly spots that would eventually eat all of her flesh. She would be unclean forever. What about Aaron? Nothing happened to him...yet he too is guilty. Miriam is distraught!

The tension builds in the room as I keep on telling the now-story. Judith anxiously moves about in her seat. Hands trembling, voice quivering Judith suddenly screams out while weeping uncontrollably: "Unfair! Unfair!" This is her story!

And Moses cried to the LORD, 'O God, please heal her—please.'

Both my prayer partner and I are weeping now, too. We too cry out to God for Judith!

> But the LORD said to Moses, 'If her father had but spit in her face, should she not be shamed seven days? Let her be shut outside the camp seven days, and after that she may be brought in again.'

Judith wept with racking sobs, her shoulders heaving. I wanted to stop and facilitate inner healing prayer right then, but God said, *Go on through*. We couldn't stop or she would not get to the root of her healing. Oh, this is painful, yet we must move through, come through the suffering with her.

> So, Miriam was shut outside the camp seven days, and the people did not set out on the march till Miriam was brought in again.

Judith's sobbing turned to wailing, piecing our own hearts with anguish. The pain was so raw. She had come to see God as an unmerciful judge, as being unfair, as One who really didn't love her. Our God is judge yes but she didn't know experientially deep inside her soul that He is also her loving Father. He is merciful and full of compassion and He sent His Son to lavish His love upon us in the midst of our sin and brokenness.

Suddenly she opened her swollen eyes, "He's here!" she said. "Jesus is right here in my tent outside the camp!" Then came the astounding revelation of Jesus healing the deep 'leprous' wound within, the sin of judging and a critical spirit she harbored in her own heart. She saw she had developed a faulty image of God as an unjust judge and realized she had been carrying that perspective all her life. Healing with her earthly father that we had prayed for before now reached a new depth of healing and forgiveness within her.

Judith cried tears of joy at being set free. Forgiveness washed her soul from her past to the present and forever. Eyes wide open with delight, like a child swept up into her father's arms, she clapped her hands.

Leaping up, and grabbing the tambourine in my office, she began to dance! Indeed she had been delivered! Singing Jewish songs with great exuberance we all danced!

> *It is for discipline that you have to endure. God is treating you as sons. For what son is there whom his father does not discipline?*
> **Hebrews 12:7**

God the Redeemer as Healer

The main thrust of Jesus' healing ministry was for healing of the body, deliverance from Satan, and proclaiming the good news. Matthew chapter nine points out physical healings done by Jesus: healing of the leper, healing the centurion's slave, healing Peter's mother-in-law. Matthew nine points to not only the evidence of Jesus healing physical illness but also healed spiritual diseases. Healing the paralytic Jesus demonstrates He has the authority to forgive sin.

"Injurious unbelief and idolatry is part of the human 'sickness' and the cycle of faith, repentance, and trusting in Jesus is the therapy bringing healing to the hurting inner person," (Coppedge, 2009, p 125). That is exactly what Jesus does!

Scripture states clearly God wants and wills everyone to be healed. What is required of us for healing to occur? Sometimes faith is the criteria for the healing. The Canaanite woman in the gospels comes to Jesus crying out for Jesus to have mercy on her daughter who is being severely oppressed by a demon. She persists and He relents pronouncing healing:

> *O woman, great is your faith! Be it done for you as you desire*
> **(Matt.15:28).**

And her daughter was healed instantly.

Sometimes our faith is not involved. People brought the sick and laid them at the feet of Jesus and they were healed with no mention of whether or not they had faith, (Matt. 15:30-31). Look at Lazarus. He was raised from the dead. Did he express faith? No, he was dead! (John 11:14). Yet he rose from the dead by the command and faith of Jesus Christ doing His Father's will. Others were healed without even asking, as the widow whose only son had died, yet Jesus filled with compassion touched the bier and commanded the young man to arise (Luke 7.14).

All healing is through Christ's sacrificial work of the redemption of humankind through the cross. The cross is the place of forgiveness of all our sins; it is the message of unconditional covenant love where the sin gap is breached. The cross is the place of resurrection and reconciliation. The work of the cross must be appropriated by each person in their lives to receive salvation for themselves. We receive salvation by faith which is based on God's faithfulness. Scriptures shows we receive healing and restoration the same way. We must take in Jesus, receive Him within.

> *Unless you eat the flesh of the Son of man and drink His blood, you have no life in yourselves. He who eats my flesh and drinks my blood has eternal life*
>
> (John 6:53-54a NAS).

The work of the cross is appropriated in every aspect of our lives; past, present and future. His life in us is healing.

Scripture is filled with healings, many of them physical but some healings involve releasing people from demonic oppression or healing other wounds inflicted psychologically or emotionally on them. Jesus publicly announced the message of His ministry this way:

> *The Spirit of the Lord is upon me, because he has anointed me to proclaim good news to the poor. He has sent me to proclaim liberty to the captives and recovering of sight to the blind, to set at liberty those who are oppressed.*
>
> Luke 4:18:

Jesus came not only to heal the physically ill or disabled but also the brokenhearted, the bruised, the downtrodden, and the ones broken by the tragedies of life in this world. Inner healing releases the heart from bondage to past traumas and hurts. The healing of one's heart involves healing the destructive power of one's negative past.

The Gospel of Mark relates the story of a young boy brought to the disciples for healing. The father said his son had a spirit that makes him mute.

> *... and whenever it seizes him, it throws him down, and he foams and grinds his teeth and becomes rigid. So I asked your disciples to cast it out, and they were not able. After Jesus rebuked his disciples He asked the father, 'How long has this been happening to him?' And he said, 'From childhood'*
>
> (Mark 9:16-27).

The question Jesus posed is about the boy's history, his past. There is a root to the demonic influence being manifested in this boy. Discovering the root cause of unhealed hurts is crucial to inner healing work in order to be set free from the negative consequences of these hurtful events.

In Scripture the sick heart is described as the source of every human, defiling, malice within us.

> *But what comes out of the mouth proceeds from the heart, and this defiles a person*
>
> (Matt. 15.18).

Inner healing is healing of the heart. It is also healing of the mind which needs renewing.

> *Do not conform to the pattern of this world but be transformed by the renewing of your mind. Then you will be able to test and approve what God's will is, His good, pleasing and perfect will*
>
> (Rom 12.2 NIV).

The Greek word for renewing encompasses complete change for the better. It is total renovation, being affected by the Holy Spirit. God wants to totally renovate you and me!

The story of the healing of Mary Magdalene at the grave of Jesus can be seen through many lenses. One lens is to see how Jesus healed her broken heart. Remember Mary Magdalene was delivered of seven demonic spirits (Luke 8:1-3). This is one who has been set free to follow Jesus. So, what happened that catapulted her back into this very dark place of despair and ungodly sorrow?

Picture Mary Magdalene as she comes to the tomb in the dimly lit morning to put spices and aromatics on her beloved Jesus. She is risking detection with the possibility of great personal harm by coming to the tomb. But this grieving, sanctified, delivered soul comes because of love. Granted she is coming looking for the dead Jesus, but it is love that draws her. Upon arrival she discovers the stone rolled away and runs to get Peter and John. Quickly they come, go inside and see the white garments of Jesus neatly folded but no body of Jesus is there.

They go home. But Mary stays still looking into the tomb. She is looking for the living among the dead.

When my father died my mother kept watching for him to appear in their apartment. She knew he had died but she kept looking for him. Mary Magdalene knew Jesus was dead for she had witnessed is death, yet she still kept looking for Him - but in the wrong place. Grief and love drove her to the tomb to look for a dead Jesus.

Marjorie (not her real name), a young woman I prayed with, had two young children die. One died by being shaken to death by someone else and the other died more recently from accidental drowning. The children's ashes lay in urns on an alter she created in her bedroom. She had built a tomb not only in her bedroom but in her heart. Since this latest tragedy, she has had another child, bringing great joy and hope into her family. Intermittently she comes for inner healing prayer work, but it is not finished. The tomb in her room is still there. She is still on the journey of healing and beginning to write about it.

While Mary Magdalene was weeping at the tomb, she stooped down and looked within like Peter and John had done, only to see two angels in white, seated at the head and foot of where Jesus' body had lain. Her response is quite amazing! The angels asked her why she was crying. Most of us would probably faint at this point or at least be speechless but not Mary. She responds,

> 'They have taken my Lord away,' she said, 'and I don't know where they have put him'
>
> (John 20.13).

Healing of the heart is a process. Mary Magdalene turns around, away from the tomb which represents grief, heartache, despair, and hopelessness and faces Jesus though she does not recognize Him. She talks with Him, questions Him, hoping for an answer from Him even though she does not know it is Him. She really thinks He's the gardener.

> See how Jesus heals her heart. First, He asks her the same question the angels asked, *'Woman, why are you crying?'*
> (John 20:13).

She releases to Him her deepest fear – which is not finding Jesus! If He is lost then so is she. Here Jesus speaks again, *'Mary.'*

She hears that voice, the voice she knows! She turns around toward him but this time with hope! She cries out in Aramaic, *Rabboni*! (which means Teacher; John 20:16). He is found, she is found, and her heart is healed through Him! The consequence of her healing is that she becomes the first evangelist of the resurrected Jesus Christ.

What do we make of healing in this story? Mary who was healed, stumbled…falling back into fear and unbelief! How could she, a sanctified, delivered, ardent and passionate follower of Jesus Christ not remember that He would rise from the dead? Why does she go looking for the living among the dead? What behavior or response do you and I default to when tragedy strikes? Is this part of the healing process too?

Mary turned from the tomb and encountered the living Jesus but did not recognize Him. She was still stuck in this worldly, ungodly sorrow that produces death.

> *For godly sorrow produces repentance leading to salvation, not to be regretted; but the sorrow of the world produces death*
> (2 Cor. 7:10).

The Greek word for sorrow connotes mourning, heaviness, grievous, and grudging grief. The difference however, is in whether the sorrow is godly or worldly. To sorrow in a godly manner leads to repentance, a change of mind, of a purpose one has formed or of something one has done. The fruit of godly sorrow is repenting, turning back to Christ. As soon as Jesus called out Mary Magdalene's name, she saw Him. "Rabboni!" she said. She was changed! She had followed Christ to the last in His humiliation at the cross and the tomb. Now she met Him first in His exaltation.

Many times people ask 'Does everyone get healed?' The conflict in healing is seen in the ideal of Jesus healing <u>every</u> disease (Matt. 4:23b) and Jesus healing <u>many</u> (Mark 1:34) and Jesus not being able to do any mighty work in Nazareth, laying His hands <u>on a few sick people and healing them</u> (Mark 6:5). All of them involve healing. How does this support, *I Am the God who heals you*?

It would appear the only way to approach this subject is to bring into focus who God is, His Word on healing, and His acts of healing with our experiences and understanding of God and healing. My assumption is it is impossible to speak about healing without a deep sense and understanding of who God is and it is impossible to speak about God without a deep sense and understanding of healing. God and healing are one. This is a challenge and one in which we will all continue to grow in knowledge, in experience and in faith. It is mysterious and awesome to enter into the character of God as Healer.

Two Bible stories demonstrate this conflict surrounding healing: 1) Paul's thorn in his side and 2) the woman with the issue of blood. Paul sought Jesus with great intensity and passion like the woman with the issue of blood.

For she said to herself, 'If only I may touch His garment, I shall be made well'

(Matt. 9:20-22)

Paul declared,

Three times I pleaded with the Lord about this, that it should leave me
(2 Cor. 12: 7-9).

Both had faith for God to heal but there were two different results: Paul's affliction stayed with him and hers was removed. What is the definition of healing here?

Look at Paul's thorn. Three times he asked God to remove it. We have no idea what this affliction was, but we do know it was grievous to Paul and caused him great discomfort. Yet he continued with even more zeal, to serve God teaching and preaching the kingdom of God in power and in authority, healing the sick and driving out demons. God had purpose in the delay of Paul's healing.

So to keep me from becoming conceited because of the surpassing greatness of the revelations, a thorn was given me in the flesh, a messenger of Satan to harass me, to keep me from becoming conceited. Three times I pleaded with the Lord about this, that it should leave me. But he said to me, 'My grace is sufficient for you, for my power is made perfect in weakness.' Therefore I will boast all the more gladly of my weaknesses, so that the power of Christ may rest upon me,

(2 Cor. 12:7-9).

Paul was healed. Was the healing of Paul a finishing of his human power in his weakness rather than a healing of an emotional or physical ailment? As I have heard my friend Rev. Nigel Mumford say at conferences: "All are healed; some are cured."

Remember healing is the very heart of God!

> *And I am sure of this, that he who began a good work in you will bring it to completion at the day of Jesus Christ and who will sustain you to the end*
>
> **(Phil. 1:6; 1Cor 1:8).**

The Greek word for completion is translated to bring to an end, accomplish, perfect, execute, complete, to take upon one's self, and to make an end for one's self.

> *...let us cleanse ourselves from every defilement of body and spirit, bringing holiness to completion in the fear of God*
>
> **(2 Cor. 7:1).**

What do these verses tell us about the process of healing? First of all it is God who began the good work of transforming and changing us into the likeness of His Son. He will be the One who brings it to completion or perfection. What lies in between the work God has begun in each of us and the completion of that work?

Song of Songs speaks to this in between time.

I have put off my coat; how shall I put it on? I have washed my feet; how shall I defile them?

(Sg. 5:3).

Relating this to inner healing, we see one who has put off the 'old man' with his unforgiveness, bitterness, and resentments. This is one who has allowed the cross of Christ to come into those past painful events where deep wounds have occurred and there forgiven the perpetrators at that deep level of wounding.

Agnes is such a one. Slowly she stands up in front of all her fellow Rwandans gathered at this healing session. She speaks in a soft but steady voice: "The men who killed my first born are here today." The silence is deafening. All wait. She moves from the microphone and by the hand brings the three men forward. All eyes are fixed on her. The men stand next to her, heads bowed. She looks intently at them as she continues: "Today I forgive you. You are my brothers."

Summation

To sum up this section is to look again at the question posed in the beginning of this chapter: Does God heal? In light of the biblical stories shared, specifically the story of Mary Magdalene we find our answer: She comes to the tomb broken with one purpose in mind, to find Jesus. She is looking for a dead Jesus, not knowing He is alive standing right behind her, waiting for her to turn back to receive healing that perhaps she did not even expect. She is not looking for healing, but she found the Healer in the midst of deep sorrow and grief and even despair (John 20:1-18). This describes the process of inner healing that occurs with many people.

Even in the pain of loss and suffering, comes the clear picture of God the Healer. Both Judith's and Agnes' testimonies confirm and testify to this truth. His very character chooses to break into our broken lives despite our lack of faith, unbelief, and knowledge of His character. God is bringing to completion the good work He began in each of us. The eschatological aspects of healing cannot be ignored for we live in the already/not yet of the kingdom of God. The kingdom of God is within and yet to come. He is the God who heals and is healing us and is bringing us through! What is God bringing you through right now?

Participants at our various healing conferences have heard my testimony of healing with my biological father that I shared at the beginning of this chapter. Some have even seen it acted out as a drama. The result is always astounding and moving as Jesus heals so many others right then and there. People who have experienced the same kind of rejection from a parent. If you who are now reading this have experienced similar rejection, know right now that Jesus is holding you and your acceptance comes from Him. Hear God's truth in your mind and heart now. You are greatly loved. Let forgiveness flow from your child-heart to the parent who rejected you or abused you or neglected you. Release that parent from your judgment. Be set free to Jesus. Feel the load of this wound you've been carrying lift off your heart. Thank Jesus right now for what He has just healed in you and He seals this healing by His own blood. Does God heal? Yes.

Chapter 2
WHAT IS INNER HEALING?

I arrived tired but excited about leading a small group at a healing conference led by Rita Bennett. The venue was just outside of Seattle, Washington. As our group gathered, I looked at each face. Some fearful, some expectant, some skeptical, some non-descript yet all seeking Gods healing touch.

As I prepared to facilitate this small group, the familiar, silent prayer arose within me: *Lord help me to see what you see; use me according to your will; let these precious people know your love; come Holy Spirit....* This is followed quickly by *help!* Aloud I prayed for us all to be protected by Christ's shed blood on the cross and then for God to give each one the desires of their hearts. And so, the healing time together began.

We shared comments about our lives, allowing questions to emerge that had been hidden inside of us for years. An older woman, whom I will call Ellen, blurted out, "I think my father molested me."

The group became very quiet. She was quite distraught about this because she explained she had withdrawn from her father years ago due to this suspicion. Her father had since died yet the buried question would not release its grip on her. In fact this question was so big inside her that she had little conscious memory of any fond childhood memories. As the Holy Spirit began to move, I prayed aloud, "Lord, lead her to a happy memory."

Negative events in a person's history can cover over joyful events of the past. Miroslav Volf (2006) writes,

> *The greater the wrong suffered the more it gets ingrained into the identity of the person who endured it. … when wrongdoing defines us, we take on distorted identities, frozen in time and closed to growth… in less severe cases the wrongdoing may not define us fully; yet it lodges in our core self and casts a dark shadow on everything we think and do" (p 79).*

As we were quietly waiting for Ellen's response, she exclaimed suddenly, "Oh I see my brother and I playing airplane in the kitchen. We have chairs all lined up in the form of a plane and I am sitting in the pilot's seat, of course, and my younger brother in the rear of the plane." In this memory she was about four years old and her brother age three. I reminded her of what Jesus stated at the end of a chapter in Matthew,

> *… and behold, I am with you always, to the end of the age,*
> **(Matthew 28:20 ESV)**

and in Hebrews we read:

> *Jesus Christ is the same yesterday, today, and forever,*
> **(Hebrews 13:8 NKJV).**

Then we know Jesus is right there in that kitchen with you and your brother as you play airplane. God is not restricted by time.

"Ask Jesus to show Himself to you in some way," I said.

Ellen exclaimed quite quickly and matter-of-factly, "Oh He is right here and I am actually sitting in His lap. Hah! We're taking off – actually flying!" God is wonderfully creative in healing I have discovered. Ellen was having a grand time in this memory until she said haltingly, "We are flying down toward a black cloud and I don't want to go there."

Immediately Jesus steered the plane away and she discovered that now He was in the pilot's seat and she was sitting behind Him with her arms wrapped around His waist much to her relief. She hadn't a clue how that exchange happened! The dark ominous cloud came up again only closer this time. I could see the fear on her face as she grimaced. I asked, "What would it take for you to let Jesus take you into and through that cloud?"

"Just sitting behind Him." She ducked behind Him like a little child does behind her mother, and immediately felt safer because she could peer out only when she wanted to. She could now face this dark scary cloud with Jesus in front of her. The uncertainty was too difficult to face alone.

This time she entered the cloud with Jesus at the controls. Gently Jesus encouraged her to look and as she did, she saw a scene in the living room of her house. Passed out on the floor completely nude was her father. He had fallen down drunk again. And in the hallway, she saw a little three year old girl, with wispy blond hair clutching her teddy bear, watching her father. She recognized it was her. Ellen said, "Oh my… he didn't do anything to me! He just passed out naked…and it scared me."

The hot tears came in torrents. Years of pent up confusion and anger were released. Here the three year-old little girl still living within her, finally gave voice to the pain that lived inside her all these years. She forgave her father from the three year-old's heart for passing out like that for her to see. Here she asked through Jesus for her daddy to forgive her for thinking he had molested her. And then in complete surrender she forgave herself for all those years of being distant from him. You see,

God is outside of time and none of these things are difficult for Him. Jesus held her and we held her as a group as the crying of the wounded little girl spent itself. The relief was huge!

"I feel like a ton has been lifted off of me!" The words rolled out while Ellen's tear stained face glowed with God's joy! And we laughed and cried with her.

This is inner healing. This is going through the cloud of uncertainty to find God's truth. The lies of the enemy were broken in her that day.

Definition of Inner Healing

It is helpful to define inner healing as we pursue greater understanding of what it is and how it works. Inner healing may be defined as God's work within the soul, bringing growth or transformative spiritual change to painful events or distorted perceptions or traumatic experiences; The process with inner healing prayer involves asking the Holy Spirit to take us to the root of the unhealed hurt, unmet need or unresolved issue that is presenting itself in the one who has come for healing. Through Jesus Christ and by the power of the Holy Spirit that event is brought to the cross where the person experiences healing. The work of Jesus Christ on the cross is appropriated to that person's life in that specific event. Inner healing prayer does not change one's past but changes a person's perspective of his or her past and the person's response to it. The person who is prayed for is set free from the pain of that memory and the negative behavioral responses that manifested from that pain. Summarizing, inner healing is a process of emotional reconstruction or transformation of spirit/soul through Jesus Christ, under the influence, direction, guidance, and power of the Holy Spirit. We witnessed this with Ellen. She went through an incredible healing which dramatically changed her whole demeanor. At the end of the healing I asked her to return to that scene and tell me what she felt.

"I have no pain," Ellen declared.

As stated previously, many people today question: *Does God heal?* What they are really asking is *Will God heal me?* Well what does God say?

I am the Lord who heals you.
(**Exodus 15:26, NIV**)

The Spirit of the Sovereign Lord is on me, because He has anointed me to preach good news to the poor. He has sent me to bind up the brokenhearted, to proclaim freedom for the captives and release from darkness for the prisoners, to proclaim the year of the Lord's favor and the day of vengeance of our God, to comfort all who mourn, and provide for those who grieve in Zion – to bestow on them a crown of beauty instead of ashes, the oil of gladness instead of mourning, and a garment of praise instead of a spirit of despair. They will be called oaks of righteousness, a planting of the Lord for the display of His splendor."
(**Isaiah 61:1-3 / Luke 4:18, NIV**)

Jesus went throughout Galilee, teaching in their synagogues, preaching the good news of the kingdom, and healing every disease and sickness among the people.
(**Matthew 4:23, NIV**)

He who was seated on the throne said, 'I am making everything new!'
(**Revelation 21:5a, NIV**)

Made in His Image

Healing is at the very heart of God! How does inner healing happen? First we need to understand the make-up of our own being. We are made in God's image – the image of the Father, Son, and Holy Spirit!

Let us make them, male and female, in our image.
(Genesis 1: 26).

The body (Greek: *soma*) is the physical part of us that receives information through the five senses: touch, smell, taste, sound, and sight. The soul (Greek: *psuche*) is comprised of our mind, will and emotions. It is the seat of the feelings, desires, affections, aversions, and heart. In the Old Testament, the Hebrew word for soul is *nephesh* which is the inner being of man, the activity of mind, activity of the will, and passion, (1 Chronicles 22:19; Psalm 23:3; Psalm 119:75; Proverbs 6:32; Matthew 10:28; John 12:27; 3 John 2). The soul is comprised of intellect, will, and emotions (Luke 22:42). Inner healing restores the soul as the psalmist declares in Psalm 23:3 *He restores my soul.* The spirit created in the image of God is renewed when we take Jesus Christ as our Savior and Lord. (Greek: *pneuma*, see scriptures Job 32:8; Proverbs 20:27; 1 Corinthians 6:19; Ecclesiastes 12:7; Ezra 11:19, 36:26; 18:31; Psalm 51:10-12; Job 32:8). But it is the spirit in man, the breath of the Almighty that gives him understanding,

Do you not know that your body is a temple of the Holy Spirit within you whom you have from God?
1Corinthisna 6:1

We further understand that God is Spirit (John 4:24) and He does not have a body or a soul. He is Spirit and only Spirit. God also has emotions, intellect, and memory and we are made in His image so we have will, emotions, intellect, and memory. We worship God from our spirit, and this indicates the ability to make decisions (will) within our spirit to worship Him. So, the soul is not the only part that has will, emotions and intellect but so does the spirit within us. We have both a will of the spirit and a will of the soul. The same is true for emotions and memory. (Kylstra & Kylstra, 2008).

The intellect is influenced by inherited temperament, and thinking and memory are the chief functions. The mind is to the emotions what food is to the body. What your mind feeds on becomes the most influential force in your life.

Our emotions or feelings are not spontaneous. They are created by what we put into our minds. You are what you read…you are what you see. What the eyes feast on forms an impression on the mind, which in turn feeds the emotions.

> *As he thinks in his heart, so is he.*
>
> **Proverbs 23:7**

The will makes us unique. The will is influenced by a person's inherited temperament (some people are strong-willed, some are weak-willed); by parental training, education and life experiences also play a role in who we are as well as what a person reads, sees and hears. Lastly, a person is unique because of the way he or she thinks and feels.

The importance of our will is that our life and eternal condition depends on it. If you choose to rebel against God, your life will constantly be in turmoil. If you surrender control of your life to God, you will enjoy fulfilment and oneness with both God and people as you travel through trials and tribulations on this earth.

There is a constant battle over who will control human thought processes – humanity, Satan or God. Sooner or later every human being makes this decision. The battle is in our minds. Who is controlling your mind?

So, this is our identity: We are made in the image of God to reflect his glory on this earth. However, that true identity can be hidden underneath layers of unhealed hurts and unmet needs. We need these hurt places and unmet needs within us healed. Why? Wounded people wound others but healed people through Jesus Christ heal others.

Healing is About Soul-Making.

What does it mean to be a soul? To be a soul is one who is fully mature and alive as a person. Everyone struggles with love yet our hope is alive because at the deepest part within us we know we are loved. To be a soul is to know that we are temporary, we are going to die physically, but live for all eternity. To be a soul means we understand the struggle for power. To be a soul is to live in both *chronos* time (sequential time) and *kairos* time (a moment of indeterminate time in which everything happens) with all its opportunities and limitations. No matter how negative our past may negatively affect our present, God has the last word. He is the One who completes the good work He began in us. We are in God's hands. Within each one's soul is a painful hole placed there by God yearning for love … His love. We erect walls around this hole in our soul. We try to camouflage it, fill it with other worthless idols and eventually deny its very existence, but love will not be denied. God's love will break through the walls or else the soul will suffocate. Love brings us naked before God and we are shocked at our barrenness. Healing is about setting our souls free through love. Jesus frees us from the prisons we have erected within ourselves either by the unhealed wounds others have inflicted on us or the unconfessed wounds we have inflicted on ourselves or others. God's love when it comes upon us, rising up through us is unwelcome at first. Why? Love scares us. It's unfamiliar. It's costly. It hurts. Yet it's who we really are becoming in God's image. We are becoming His unconditional love. Lord, break open our hearts now and that we may receive!

Process of Inner Healing

How does inner healing happen, especially of past events? The first critical theological and Biblical understanding is:

> *Jesus is the same yesterday and today and forever.*
> **(Hebrews 13: 8, NIV).**

The second truth follows:

> *Therefore, if anyone is in Christ, he is a new creation; the old has gone, the new has come! All this is from God, who reconciled us to himself through Christ and gave us the ministry of reconciliation: that God was reconciling the world to himself in Christ, not counting men's sins against them. And he has committed to us the message of reconciliation.*
> **(2 Corinthians 5:17-19, NIV).**

> *the eternal God is a dwelling place. And underneath are his everlasting arms;*
> **(Deuteronomy 33:27).**

And lastly,

> *I am with you always, to the end of the age,*
> **(Matthew 28:20)**

Jesus is outside of time because He is eternal and therefore, He is with us in our past, present, and all eternity. Jesus is present in every event, even the milliseconds of our lives, for He never left us and never will. God can heal anything that has negatively impacted us in our lives or is currently happening in our lives. If something in our past wounded us and we still experience pain today, it is not past at all. Sometimes the effects of past wounding shows up in different ways. These side effects can be debilitating and keep us imprisoned by fear or lack of trust or any other variety of negative reactions.

I was nearly kidnapped as a four year-old child playing with a friend in an alley in the back of my inner-city, row house. By the grace of God my aunt who was visiting from North Carolina rescued me and my little friend from a man's car we had climbed into after he offered us a fun ride. While inside his car, I had been frightened badly by this man and cried all the way as we ran home with my aunt. You see the man had exposed himself to me and in those days, no one really talked about these things. The police looked for him and I remember my daddy walking me to kindergarten every day the rest of that year. I still can feel my little hand in his as we walked. I was safe. How did this unhealed wounding negatively impact my life? I became afraid of the dark. I had to have music on and a light in order to fall asleep. That fear of the dark continued into adulthood until I was healed of that trauma. How did Jesus do that?

As a prayer person prayed with me, immediately I was taken to that scene where my friend and I got into a strange man's car. Jesus, who has always been with me, shows me He is there in the scene as this man tries to take us away. My little friend and I are in the front seat and Jesus is in the back seat. The man left the car locking us in to get something from his house. I was crying, frightened by the sexual exposure and advance he made toward me. My aunt who was looking for me came running when she saw two little heads in this big black car parked up the alley. The locks in the car were so big and hard to pull up with our little fingers. We couldn't do it. Suddenly Jesus' fingers wrapped around ours pulling the lock up…I saw Him do it! We jumped out of the car and ran home with my aunt. Then Jesus took me to my bedroom and His light filled it. All the darkness had to flee for even the darkness is as light to God! There in the midst of His light He cleansed and washed me in His love. He healed the terrible image that had remained in my mind all these years. Jesus healed my soul and my body. Through Jesus I forgave this man for what he had done. And I prayed that he had found Jesus Christ and been healed himself. Freedom came into my life and I no longer needed the night light nor the music to sleep at night. I have Jesus! Alleluia!

Inner Child

Many of our wounds can be traced back to childhood. So, it is our inner child who needs the healing even though we are grown. All the memories of past events and emotions that took place during the first seven years of your life including the womb, are recorded on the hard drive of your inner child.

We have within us a creative child and a hurt child. Rita Bennett (1998) puts it this way:

The creative child is made up of all the healed and healthy attitudes and memories of your early life than can help you to be open, loving, quick to forgive, trusting, imaginative, spontaneous, creative, playful, inquisitive, unaffected, free, willing to try new things, and responsive.

Rita Bennett (2004) further explains:

The hurt child is made up of the unhealed attitudes, memories, and reactions to those memories which sometimes cause us to regress to negative childhood behavior. The more injured a person is, the more often he will find himself feeling and acting like this hurt child. The childish adult may throw temper tantrums to get control, pout, speak in childish whiny voice, cry to get his way, throw things, be extremely self-centered, think the world revolves around him, avoid responsibility, run away, resist change, take refuge in fantasy.

The root causes in the hurt child come from unhealed hurts, traumas, unmet needs, unforgiveness, and other hurtful issues in one's past. The negative 'fruit' or behavior we see in our adult life comes from these 'root' causes.

Jesus asked the boy's father, 'How long has he been like this?' 'From childhood,' he answered

(Mark 9:21).

The boy in this healing event had a spirit that seized him, throwing him down on the ground. The boy foamed and clenched his teeth and became rigid. The father had asked the disciples to cast it out and they couldn't. They brought the boy to Jesus and He asked the father how long this had been going on.

In other words Jesus is asking what the source of this boy's behavior is. When did this begin? We can also ask what the sources of the emotional wounds are in someone. The sources are unhealed hurts, unmet needs, and unresolved issues. Unhealed hurts are birthed whenever we lose something good that we had received and needed to be whole and healthy. Unmet needs are birthed when we do not get all that we needed to be whole. Unresolved issues are birthed when we do not know how to productively process our unmet needs and unhealed hurts. (Savard, 2002). We can also ask if anyone else in the family, looking at past generations, exhibited this behavior.

Summation

Our identification is either in God or in the sin that has been delivered from us. Once the sin is delivered from us it loses the power to name us. Inner healing of the unhealed hurts and the unmet needs takes away the power of these negative events. They can no longer label or name us. We are named by God.

> *No longer will they call you Deserted or name your land Desolate. But you will be called Hephzibah (the City of Gods Delight) and your land Beulah (The Bride of God); for the Lord will take delight in you, and your land will be married."*
>
> (Isaiah 62:4 NIV).

> *Do not be afraid for I have redeemed you; I have called you by name, you are mine.*
>
> (Isaiah 43:1 ESV)

As Christians we believe that neither what we do nor what we suffer defines us at the deepest level. *We are defined by the flame of God's presence which gives us new identity that burns in us inextinguishably. Our bodies and souls are the temples of the Lord and 'though our bodies and souls may become ravaged yet we continue to be God's temple – at times a temple in ruins, but sacred space nonetheless.'* (Volf, 2006, p79)

Today we ask ourselves: What kind of person do you think you are? What kind of person do you think you are becoming?

Pray these scriptures aloud over yourself:

I AM

I am made in God's image (Gen 1:26)

I am born of God (1 John 5:18)

I am led by the Spirit of the Living God (Romans 8:14)

I am a temple of the Holy Spirit (1 Cor 6:19)

I am not my own (1Cor. 1:19)

I am bought with a price (1 Cor. 7:23)

I am full of the love of God (Rom. 5:5)

I am forgiven (Col 1:14)

I am walking in love (Eph. 5:2)

I am at peace with God through my Lord Jesus Christ (Rom. 5:1)

I am fully persuaded what He's promised, He's able to do (Rom 4:21)

I am not under the law, but under grace (Rom. 6:16)

I am free from the law of sin and death (Rom 8:2)

I am walking in the newness of the spirit (Rom. 7:6)

I am giving my Father joy because I'm walking in truth. (1 John 1:14)

I am worth the body and blood of Jesus (Luke 22:18-19):

I am receiving the unconditional love of God (Rom 5:8)

I am seated in heavenly places in Christ Jesus (Eph 2:6)

I am a saint (Eph 1:1)

I am accepted (Eph 1:6)

I am greatly loved. (Daniel 10:19)

I am precious in the sight of the Lord (Ps. 116:16)

I am a servant (Ps 116:1)

I am listened to by God my Father (Ps 116:1)

I am dead to sin (Romans 6:11)

I am alive unto God through Jesus Christ my Lord (Romans 6:11)

I am free from condemnation (Rom 8:1)

I am giving thanks in all things (Phil 4:6)

I am laying aside all malice, envy, evil speaking (1 Peter 2:1)

I am partaking of God's divine nature (1 Peter 2:1)

I am not a victim, but an overcomer (Rev 12:11)

I am fashioned by the Master's hand (Eph. 2:10)

I am a value to God (Matt 10:31)

I am walking in great peace, because I love God's law (of love) and nothing does offend me (Ps 119:165)

I am predestined to be conformed to the image of His Son (Rom 8:29)

I am wise in heart (Prov 10:8)

I am an overcomer by the blood of the Lamb and the word of my testimony (Rom 12:11)

I am healed by His stripes (Is 53:5)

I am strong in the Lord and power of His might (Eph 6:10)

Taken from "The I AM Book" Copyright Susan Eaves
P.O. Box 19745
Sarasota, Florida 34278 used with permission

Chapter 3
HEALING UNHEALED HURTS AND UNMET NEEDS

"Can you meet with my son? He's so angry! And he's hurting his little brother. We just don't know what to do and he said he'd come and talk with you, Pastor Sharon," the distraught mother asked. The next day, Charles (not his real name) walked in the door. At eleven he was already a strapping, good looking, interracial boy. He had been adopted at birth. At the time he was adopted the adoptive parents could not legally have him until the third day after he was born.

As Charles and I sat down at the table I asked him to draw his heart for me. Quickly he worked creating the outline of a heart then grabbing the black crayon he began to fill in the heart with vigorous strokes.

"What's that, Charles?" I asked.

"I'm sad," he responded while grabbing up the red crayon and furiously coloring in the rest of the heart.

"What's that, Charles?" I followed up.

"I'm angry…very angry", he said raising his voice a bit.

After talking about that briefly I suggested we take this to Jesus to find out the root of this sadness and anger. Closing his eyes, Charles immediately saw a picture, which he described as though a movie was unfolding before his eyes. "I see Jesus handing me to my birth mother and she's smiling at me. That's pretty neat," he said with a grin. He was quiet again for a while until he shared, "I'm in a lonely place...I don't like it. I'm scared." His voice was quivering, and he was visibly upset.

I knew we had to go through this so I prayed, *Lord Jesus show him the truth.*

Quite suddenly he exclaimed, "That was a lie! A lie!...I was not all alone...Jesus is carrying me into the nursery room and staying with me the whole time...oh wow! Now He is carrying me to my parents! Geez Mom is crying and dad is laughing!"

By this time Charles and I both were crying and laughing! Jesus broke the power of the lie of the enemy that had been whispered in his baby ears, *you are all alone.* Satan is such a liar!

Since forgiveness is paramount to healing success, Charles forgave his birth mother for giving him away though he actually felt quite good about that. He forgave his mom and dad for not getting him right away when I told him they weren't allowed to do that for three days. It wasn't because they didn't want him, it was because they were held back. He forgave himself for holding onto this for so long and he repented and asked forgiveness with Jesus and me as his pastor for all his angry outbursts he had shown to his parents and little brother. He did this later with them in person.

"Charles," I asked, "would you draw your heart again?" He drew a big heart and colored it all in red. A little concerned I asked, "What's that?"

He looked at me the way only eleven year old boys can when they know they are right about something and speaking with great assurance said, "That's the blood of Jesus in my heart!" Selah! (Hebrew word for 'pause'!) We sealed that healing in the name of the Father, Son and Holy Spirit and with a quick hug and his rolled-up heart drawing clutched in his hand out the door he bolted.

His mother told me later that his angry outbursts had diminished greatly after this healing prayer. There were other times his anger had to be dealt with as he grew up but exposing and healing that root cause initiated deeper healing later on in his life which gave him the freedom to change his behaviors.

Unhealed hurts are birthed whenever we lose something good and needed to be whole and healthy. Some things we can temporarily lose are our true identity, hope, acceptance, and love. Many times we deal with these losses by dysfunctional behaviors. Behaviors such as unforgiveness and addictions block our healing. These unhealed losses become blocks to healing.

It is the soul that is in need of healing. Hidden in the mind, will and emotions of the soul are the hurt areas that set off people's negative and even destructive reactions. It is here in the soul that healing needs to take place. This is where the unhealed hurts live in you.

Inner Child

Remember within you lives your inner child. Your inner child includes all that you have learned and experienced, especially during your first seven years. All your memories and emotions are recorded on your inner hard drive, including your prenatal existence. That inner child is part of you today and within that inner child is the creative child and the hurt child (See Chapter 2). This is where inner healing occurs.

And He said: "I tell you the truth, unless you change and become like little children, you will never enter the kingdom of heaven."
(Matthew 18:3)

When I was a child, I talked as a child, I thought like a child, I reasoned like a child. When I became a man, I put childish ways behind me.
(1 Corinthians 13:11)

Root Causes

'Root cause' or 'first cause' refers to the initial incident when the emotional hurt or when the destructive lie was first believed. Another way of expressing the root cause is to speak about when the gate in our soul was opened for the enemy's destructive and harmful influence.

Remember Jesus gives us the Scriptural basis for this concept of root causes:

Jesus asked the boy's father, 'How long has he been like this?'... 'From childhood,' he answered.
Mark 9: 21

Jesus demonstrated the importance of knowing the initial causes of a problem. If the inner healing can occur at the initial place of incidence, then all subsequent reactions and behaviors can be healed more easily as well. Many times, dealing with the root-cause incident will actually heal all later related occurrences.

Another way to express this concept of root causes is to 'follow the fruit to the root.' If we observe people with positive behaviors, positive attitudes, even good physical health the roots can be traced back to healthy childhood experiences which include affirmation, showing of affection, good values in upbringing and good physical care. Likewise when we observe negative behaviors, negative attitudes, anxiety, fears, unwillingness to forgive, inability to share, and even many physical illnesses, you can find the roots in these past unhealed areas - traumas, unmet needs and times when the needed love and parental nurturing was missing.

How do we discover the root causes of the negative behavior in a person's life? First of all, we do not dig around in someone's past looking for the root cause of their unresolved issues. Remember this is all God's work. We begin by asking the Holy Spirit to bring up a memory of an issue where this negative behavior, uncomfortable feeling, or physical illness occurred. We wait for the Holy Spirit to reveal this. We can ask questions of the person who has come for prayer that may help the root to be revealed.

Examples of questions to ask:
1. Who do you feel first loved you? Not who should have loved you but who did you feel loved you? Another way of asking this, is *'Who lights up when you walk in the room?'*
2. If the person presents an anxious or fearful feeling, I often ask, *'When have you felt this before?'*
3. Perhaps the person states, *I'm just not good enough* or *Whatever I do it's never enough.* You can then ask: *How long have you believed that?* or *Did someone ever say that to you?*
4. Other good questions include: *"What is your first fearful memory?"* and *What is a happy memory from your childhood?*

I was leading a small group at a healing conference and in my group was one of the saddest men I had ever met. His whole countenance was down! Even his mouth was turned down and the light in his eyes was barely visible. I had discovered through the intake paperwork, that he was terribly physically and emotionally abused by his father. When it was his turn to introduce himself in the group he said, "I have been depressed all my life."

Everyone was silent, not knowing what to do. The Holy Spirit challenged that statement he made as I asked, "When was your first happy memory?"

He looked at me in shock as if to say *'didn't you hear me?'* Off guard for a moment he blurted, "Oh I can see my cousin and I at a family picnic and we are having such fun!" He was actually grinning at this point! Closing his eyes and entering this scene he described the activity going on: "We are throwing logs into the river, watching them float downstream."

I reminded him that Jesus says *I AM with you always*, and then I asked, "Where is Jesus?"

He laughed...yes he laughed, "He's throwing logs in with us too!" What a joy for him to see Jesus playing with him and his cousin with full abandonment!

But suddenly his demeanor changed to fear, "My father is yelling at us to stop."

I encouraged him to keep his eyes on Jesus and stay behind Him. "He's talking to my father...He has his hand on my father's shoulder..." I could tell how shocked he was to observe this. Jesus turned around and beckoned him to come closer. He did while making sure to stay behind Jesus. He overhears his father telling Jesus that he is concerned that the logs will pile up further down the stream causing a jam up. Jesus agrees. Apparently, there were times his father was caring and not abusive. His father's drinking usually led to the abusive episodes.

In this particular memory, hope was restored and the lie of the enemy, that had kept him depressed was broken. By the power of the Holy Spirit we now pulled out the root of depression breaking the negative power and influence of this root on his life. This healing enabled him to begin the process of forgiving his father. A noticeable change could be seen in his face and eyes! The whole group saw his mouth turn up and a glimmer of light fill his eyes! How amazing is our God! Through inner healing the countenance of the Lord buried deep within him, was now shining out of him. He had more healing work to do but God now had broken through the log jam of lies Satan had told him and he was on the journey to becoming whole.

The truth of God's word!

Jesus is the same yesterday, today, and forever.
(Hebrews 13:8)

Where can I go from Your Spirit? Where can I flee from your presence? ..l For you created my innermost being; You knit me together in my mother's womb. I praise you because I am fearfully and wonderfully made... All the days ordained for me were written in your book before one of them came to be.
(Psalm 139: 7, 13-14, 16)

The Lord himself goes before you and will be with you; He will never leave you nor forsake you. Do not be afraid; do not be discouraged.
(Deuteronomy 31:8)

And surely I am with you always, to the very end of the age.
(Matthew 28:20b)

Kinds of Soul Healing Prayer

God is a creative and miracle-working God. He heals in any manner that He chooses. For this reason, it is critical that prayer facilitators be totally submitted to the work of the Holy Spirit, not following their own agendas or expectations nor even methods of healing they have learned over the years. One never knows when God will do something brand new.

There are four types of inner healing (or soul healing) prayer: (1) healing of a memory prayer, (2) happy memory prayer, (3) creative prayer and (4) dispelling lies. They each represent a framework for God's creative intervention that will often be expansive and multi-faceted in nature. God cannot be boxed-in when we are submitted to His plan and purpose.

Healing of a Memory Prayer

An inner healing prayer experience is one where the person being prayed for responds to a memory that is revealed by the Holy Spirit. The person recounts briefly the circumstances of the particular memory. They may sense and acknowledge the pain, the hurt, negative feelings, or false belief that the Holy Spirit reveals. In the course of the prayer, Jesus makes His Presence known in the memory. In some way the person sees, hears, feels, senses, or knows by faith Jesus is present. A new perspective is gained through Jesus, allowing a new truth to be revealed, forgiveness to be released, and healing to come. The past event is still a fact (*it happened*), but the perspective of that memory has changed in the presence of Jesus. Ask the person to revisit the memory just prayed about. Ask what they are feeling or sensing. Usually the pain is no longer felt in association with the memory. If pain is still there, continue with inner healing prayer asking the Holy Spirit to show what is blocking the healing.

Happy Memory Prayer

There are times when the Holy Spirit brings to mind a happy memory. This is often in order for the person being prayed for to remember and feel safe, carefree, protected, nurtured, or any other positive feeling or belief that such a memory would foster. Jesus' presence is noted in the memory in whatever way that He chooses to manifest Himself (sight, sound, feel, smell, or by faith). The validation received in the positive memory may bring healing in and of itself. Healing comes just being in Jesus' presence. Sometimes the Lord may use a happy memory before bringing forth a more difficult memory that has to be dealt with.

Creative Prayer

In following the Holy Spirit's lead, the person may experience a creative event or revelation that is not an actual memory or real-life event. The Lord creatively demonstrates a truth or understanding in the creative prayer experience. Healing comes as a result of this supernatural prayer experience with the Lord. I have seen the Lord do this in cases where a person has been sexually abused.

> *"For My thoughts are not your thoughts, neither are your ways My ways," declares the Lord. "As the heavens are higher than the earth, so are My ways higher than your ways and my thoughts than your thoughts."*
> (Isaiah 55:8-9)

Dispelling Lies

In this form of inner healing prayer, the individual being prayed for expresses beliefs that have been present in specific or general life circumstances. False beliefs are identified and root causes (open gates) are sought through the Holy Spirit. Many times the person may go back to a specific memory. Jesus is asked to reveal His truth. The participant asks for forgiveness from Jesus for believing the lie and forgives others for instilling or continuing the lie-based belief and usually the participant needs to forgive him or herself.

> *Then you will know the truth, and the truth will set you free.*
> (John 8:32)

Renouncing Past Behaviors and Practices

With the help of the Holy Spirit, people may become aware of behaviors, beliefs, or ritualistic practices they have been involved in that even now continue to have a negative hold on their lives. Once brought to mind, these negative influences can be renounced which means to willfully act to give up, abandon, or disown a spirit or behavior that does not bring glory to God. Renouncing is an open declaration or proclamation of one's intent to change. Renouncing is done by the person who is receiving prayer in the Name of Jesus and by His authority. Forgiveness is asked of the Lord for having ever participated in the wrong behavior or belief. Prayer facilitators pray in agreement with the one giving up the past behavior or belief. Together in prayer they affirm the gifts of God's mercy and grace for the individual. Prayer facilitators pray that the Holy Spirit fill and dwell in all places in the individual that have been emptied through the renouncing prayer.

A strong young Christian woman came to me for inner healing prayer. Even though she had been healed deeply of aberrant sexual behaviors of her past, there was still a lingering pain. I liken it to when one downs a full glass of milk, a residue or film of milk remains inside the glass. There was a residue of regret for this past behavior lingering in her heart. I picked up my *Book of Common Prayer* (BCP) and there, in my living room, we both knelt and began the ancient rite of confession. *Bless me, for I have sinned.* (BCP, 1982, p 447). And here, in the presence of Christ and me, her minister, she humbly and obediently confessed her sins to Almighty God, her Creator and Redeemer (BCP, 1982, p 450). His mercy filled the room as we both wept. As she turned her whole soul to Christ once again, in every part of her life, past, present, and future, forgiveness flowed washing her inside out. Placing my hands on her head I prayed, "May Almighty God in mercy receive your confession of sorrow and of faith, strengthen you in all goodness, and by the power of the Holy Spirit keep you in eternal life" (BCP, 1982, p. 451). We broke out with rejoicing and I know it broke out in heaven too! Later she said she had never thought to confess it out openly like that. The residue of regret was gone!

> *Therefore, confess your sins to one another and pray for one another, that you may be healed.*
>
> (James 5:16a ESV)

Examples of these past behaviors, patterns, or wrong choices are:

<u>Cults</u>: Any belief that is not a Judeo-Christian belief. Instead, it teaches that there is some other way to heaven than through Jesus Christ and does not profess Jesus as the Son of God. (*See Micah 4:5 and 1 John 4:1-2*)

<u>The Occults</u>: Pertains to magic, astrology, and other alleged sciences, or groups that practice these sciences, claiming to seek, manipulate, or use information obtained from the spiritual world for their own purposes which are often evil. (*See Deuteronomy. 18:9-14, Acts 19:19*)

<u>Sexual Involvement</u>: Inappropriate, illicit involvement in sexual activity outside of marriage; perverted or deviant sexual activities; pornography, unbiblical sexual behavior. (*See Leviticus 18, 1 Corinthians 6:18, Romans1:26-32*)

<u>Addictions</u>: Compulsive dependence on drugs, alcohol, relationships, or behaviors that take precedence in our lives, removing God from His rightful place in our hearts; addictive behaviors become idols. (*See Romans 1:25; 7:14: -25, 1 Corinthians 6:19*)

In conclusion in dealing with healing unhealed hurts, unmet needs and unresolved issues, always remember the first healing is salvation. Salvation restores our relationship with God by opening up access to the Father through the death and resurrection of His Son, Jesus Christ and through the power of the Holy Spirit. Sins are paid for, debts are cancelled, and new life is given to us. Alleluia! And scripture exhorts us to *work out our salvation in fear and trembling*, (Philippians 2:12). We are saved and we need the healing of our soul.

Inner healing of our soul (mind, will, emotions) allows this relationship with God to grow deeper as God draws us to Himself, forgiving and taking our sins, healing past hurts, filling unmet needs, resolving issues in our lives, dismantling the lies of the enemy, and breaking bondages that have kept us from walking in the fullness of all that He has for us. Not only is the guilt removed from the darkness we once walked in but so is the shame and unforgiveness. Freedom comes for us and for others in our lives. In this process of healing the work of the cross of Christ is being appropriated in us.

We have a saying in this ministry that *wounded people wound others, and healed people through Jesus Christ heal others.*

We are called to be healers and reconcilers with Jesus Christ. It begins with our own healing first and then goes forth to others! This is playing the Gospel of Jesus Christ forward!

*"The Spirit of the Sovereign Lord is on me,
because the Lord anointed me
to preach good news to the poor.
He has sent me to bind up the brokenhearted,
to proclaim freedom for the captives
and release from darkness for the prisoners."*

- Isaiah 61: 1 –

Chapter 4
BLOCKS TO HEALING: IDENTITY ISSUES SLUMBERING SPIRIT

Identity

We drive up the steep narrow streets of Jicamarca, Peru in our packed van. Excitement grows as we near the cement pad carved out of the mountain. The people, who live here, labored long and hard to make it for their children to play on. The way of life here is hard. The first thing I notice is the lack of greenery. Dusty brown dirt and gravel cover the landscape but just as stunning are the shacks painted in pastel colors, built on the precarious side of the mountain! The people have also built wooden stairs going straight up the mountain – stairs which the children navigate easily as they come scampering down the mountain to greet us. Many of the little girls wear long dresses or skirts. One beautiful child face after another gathers on the cement pad in anticipation! They know juice and sweets are coming. They know a team from the church is here again to sing and dance with them and tell them stories about Jesus. All the stray dogs are scrambling down too. Many are emaciated but they come hoping for scraps of food or even a pat on their heads.

At one point I am called to lead the children into a healing encounter with Jesus. Standing in front of these beautiful children, with upturned expectant faces staring at me, I asked them, "What do you want Jesus to do for you?"

The answers come quickly,
"To stop my daddy drinking."
"To get along with my mother."
"To have more food,"

A little ten-year-old girl sitting in the middle of the group spoke softly: "To make me pretty. I am ugly."

My heart sank within me for her wounded heart at such a young tender age. Her broken image of herself was etched in her sorrowful face and cast down eyes.

I asked them all to close their eyes and ask Jesus to come. I prayed, "Lord Jesus, come and meet each child in their wounded place and heal them. May each one meet you Jesus."

I could see eyes fluttering beneath their closed eyelids, and I knew Holy Spirit was moving. Smiles began to break out on their beautiful, olive-skinned faces as Jesus touched their hearts, healing wounds I knew nothing about but that didn't matter because God did. When the prayer session ended and while one of the staff led them in a praise song, I asked this little ten-year-old old girl to come aside with me and our translator. The little girl told me her mother had called her ugly. With her eyes closed I prayed, "Come Lord Jesus and show yourself to this precious girl and tell her your truth."

Suddenly her eyes popped wide open, "He called me princess! He said I am pretty!" Tears streamed down her face and mine too. One of the teenagers came over and wrapped her arms around her, filling her with love and affirmation. The little girl's older sister joined us too. With a glowing face and up-lifted heart the little girl ran back to join her friends. As we were pulling out at the end of this blessed time with these precious children of God, she came running up to the van. "Gracias! Gracias Pastora!" she exclaimed. I noticed her head was down.

I said, "Lift up your head, Princess. This is who you are now in Christ. Walk as royalty, Princess, in the kingdom of God!" She straightened up and the biggest smile erupted on her face! Time and time again a person's true identity is restored by Jesus Christ in inner healing.

While working on my doctoral thesis on relapse in inner healing, I recruited volunteers for my research. From them I heard first-hand the necessity for further healing. There was still work to be done in the healing of their true identity in Christ and not the identity of their past wounds, sins or what others think. This need for the healing of wounded identities was expressed by some participants in the study I conducted:

My presenting issue of healing that continues to bother me is "they do not like me and I am not good enough.

They don't like me... Why don't they like me?

I feel a lack in myself – not doing enough. There is always a feeling that, 'I am a disappointment'.

What is our identity and what does this have to do with the inner healing of our souls?

- Child of God - (John 1:12; 1 John 3:1-2)
- Adopted - (Ephesians 1:5)
- Accepted - (Romans 15:7)
- Given fullness in Christ - (Colossians 2:9-10)
- United with the Lord - (1 Corinthians 6:17)
- No longer slaves to sin - (Romans 6:6)
- Created in Gods image - (Genesis 1:27)
- God formed you - (Jeremiah 1:5)

- A fearfully and wonderfully made child of God – (Psalm 139:14)
- Called by you name – (Isaiah 43:1; John 10:3)
- God's plan for your life – (Jeremiah 29:11)
- New creation in Christ Jesus – (2 Corinthians 5: 17)
- You are a part of the Body of Christ - (1 Corinthians 12:27)
- A chosen people - (1 Peter 2:9)
- Baptized into Christ & clothed with Christ - (Galatians 3:27-28)
- Your body is the temple of the Holy Spirit - (1 Corinthians 6:19-20)
- Raised with Christ - (Colossians 3:1-3)
- Made alive in Christ – (Ephesians 2: 4-6)

In whom or in what do we find our identity? The understanding of self is found in the image of the triune God revealed specifically in Jesus Christ. This is the acceptance of our true self made in the image of God manifested in Christ Jesus.

What blocks self-acceptance of our true self? "The unredeemed mind of man split off from the mind of the Creator, denies its Origin, denies itself," (Barth, 1982, p54). This refers to those who do not know Christ but can also refer to areas of our mind not yet relinquished to Christ. How does this happen? Karl Barth sees this contradiction of self as a battle between the *'Yes'* and the *'No'* that resides in our soul. The *'Yes'* is the saved and healed areas in our soul and the *'No'* is the flesh part of us not yet healed or surrendered fully to God. As Christians we belong to the *'Yes'* of God even though the rebellious *'No'* still battles within us. Paul confirms this ongoing battle within when he states he is the foremost sinner of all (1 Timothy 1:15) and the painful lament:

I do not understand what I do. For what I want to do, I do not do, but what I hate to do, I do... I have the desire to do what is good but I cannot carry it out

(Romans 7:15)

The *'No'*, the flesh, is our fallen nature. At times the *'No'* in us has had greater power temporarily to rule our lives than the *'Yes'* has but it cannot erase this *'Yes'* of God in us. This speaks succinctly about the conflict within us and the process of inner healing.

The knowledge of God is the starting point for healing. In coming to know God we begin to face the conflict that is going on inside our souls. This conflict in the Gospel story of the father of the boy afflicted by a mute spirit who cried, *'Lord, I believe; help my unbelief* (Mark 9.24). We are dust and ashes. We start out in life made in God's image yet somewhere along the line, we stop believing this. Our true identity begins to be covered over with the ashes of sin and the dirt of infected inner wounds. We can actually experience a relapse in believing that our identity is in God, our Creator. Is the truth, *'I am made in His image'* and *'I am not yet perfected'* the root of the struggle for identity that at the root when we are tempted to return to old destructive behavior patterns that have been subjected to the healing process in Christ?

Our identification is either in God or it is in our sin. Once we are healed and forgiven of our own sin or sins committed against us through the work of the cross, that sin loses the power to name us. However,

> *The greater the wrong suffered the more it gets ingrained into the identity of the person who endured it. …when wrongdoing defines us, we take on distorted identities, frozen in time and closed to growth… in less severe cases the wrongdoing may not define us fully; yet it lodges in our core self and casts a dark shadow on everything we think and do (Volf, 2006, p79).*

As Christians we believe that neither what we do nor what we suffer defines us at the deepest level. We are defined by the inextinguishable flame of God's presence in us which gives us a new identity. Our bodies and souls are the temples of the Lord and

...though our bodies and souls may become ravaged yet we continue to be God's temple – at times a temple in ruins, but sacred space nonetheless. (Volf, 2006, 79).

Our true identification is in God. Identity is our individuality, our character and original distinctiveness as created in God's image. It's our ID. It is a condition of being oneself and not another. Today some people have had their identities stolen. Bank accounts have been cleaned out and people have lost their good credit because someone robbed their identity through fraudulent means. Others had their identity stolen by unfounded, libelous accusations and good names have been destroyed. Behind all identity theft is Satan himself. He has come to steal, kill and destroy our core being. But praise God, he cannot do that because we have been saved by grace, forgiven and redeemed through the shed blood of Jesus Christ. Sin still has power but only in areas in our soul that are unhealed. Once sin is delivered from us it loses its power.

Identity Theft

The theft of our true identity in God has actually been going on for years. Our identity is stolen by the power sin has in us. Working in inner healing ministry, I observe people struggling between their identification in God and in the sin from which they were delivered. The reason being they have not yet been fully healed in their soul. These struggles can continue even after healing of hurtful past events has occurred. Why? Sometimes there are layers of healing that must happen within us. Sometimes it is a generational issue that must be addressed. For some people the battle within can result in relapses observable by the return of negative behavior. God's enemy, Satan and the world try to steal your identity. How does this happen?

- Lies you are told about yourself and you believe like the little girl in Peru.
- Hurts that leave you wounded and afraid.
- Unmet needs that make you feel forgotten, not worth anything, invisible.
- Comparisons that make you feel "less than" who you are.
- What others expect you to be or expectations we have of ourselves.
- Labels you are given: victim, orphan, widow, killer, and so on..

We yearn to know who we are and whose we are. At the tender age of twelve, I discovered quite by accident a horrible fact. It rocked my identity and my world. As I was cleaning our red Pontiac convertible for Mom and Dad, I saw a paper partially sticking out of the glove compartment. With full intent of just cramming it back into the glove compartment something on the paper caught my eye. The name on the certificate read: Sharon Lynn Youngs. Who is that? I wondered who that was so I read on a bit. The certificate stated that Joseph J Gottfried, my dad, adopts Sharon Lynn Youngs. It was dated back to when I was three years old. I read it again hardly believing my eyes. I will never forget gasping for breath. *What?! I am adopted?!* Tears flowing down my face and anger rising, I screamed: "My dad isn't my dad?!" I loved him so much! Why I use to get up early on Saturday mornings and run the milk route with him. He always bought me jelly donuts along the way! We fished together; I sat in his lap, his big blue eyes holding back tears of love as he looked at me. *Not my dad? …Who am I? What is wrong with me? They lied…* I didn't speak to my father for at least a year because I was heartbroken. Of course, I eventually did talk to him and life went on, though a bit differently for the deep hurt remained. The buried scar of rejection as a baby by my biological father who I never knew was now freshly opened, like an exposed nerve. In the ensuing years healing took place at surface levels but not at the root until I was introduced to inner healing prayer work. Then I discovered my true identity in Christ, my Lord and Savior.

How do you go through the wilderness of healing? How do you go through the wilderness of rejection? Abandonment by any parent fosters negative thinking about one's self. Sometimes orphaned children, even those who have been adopted, see themselves as cast offs, throw-a-ways, unlovable, someone who was not wanted by their mother or father. If the root of these false labels is not healed this orphan spirit will continue to manifest itself destructively especially in present relationships. These old wounds are easily pricked by the newest hurtful event.

Isabelle was a young, beautiful, Rwandan widow with five children. When the Rwandan genocide occurred in 1994 she was about ten years old and her entire family was killed. She was left an orphan with no surviving family members. Hope for healing brought her to our conference. She barely spoke above a whisper as she explained that the way she fed her children was to ask neighbors if she could dig in their gardens after they had gathered their own harvest. They gave permission and whatever she found she could sell and also feed her children. This is how she was surviving.

"May I pray with you?" I quietly asked. Inwardly I groaned with such heart ache. I prayed for Jesus to manifest Himself right there with her. I noticed a slight movement of her head. "Is Jesus with you right now?" gently prodding. She nodded yes. Taking another deep breath I asked Jesus to reveal her true identity.

Then I saw a tear coming down her face...then another and another. Quiet sobbing ensued as she said, "I am not an orphan." I waited for what seemed an interminably long time until she spoke again, "I am child of God." Her shy grin turned into a smile that flooded her face. It was the greatest gift of God that day. He showed her there are no orphans in the kingdom of Heaven. All are in the family of God.

Two years later on our third healing mission trip to Rwanda, we went back to her town again and gathered with all the men and women. I was seated on the platform with the other Anglican African priests. After a joyous, hand clapping, dancing, singing worship time we sat down to hear testimonies. A beautiful young woman stood up to share her testimony of what she had gone through in the genocide and how God has healed her. She was tall, elegant, regal in stature and very confident. Her words were strong.

Father Philbert leaned over and whispered, "That is Isabelle."

What? I had not even recognized her! Tears of great joy and gratitude began to stream down my face as I watched and listened to her testimony! Such a dramatic difference! Later she was also part of the woman s dance team. As she glided by me with such grace, she just looked at me smiling so broadly with a twinkle in her eye. She knew I was stunned! I preached that afternoon on the Woman at the Well who after receiving the living words of life, leaves her water jug behind, the old past and its shame, and runs with great joy to tell her friends that she has just met the One who told her everything about her life…Jesus Christ. Isabelle has indeed left her water jug filled with tears of loss, shame, hopelessness, abandonment and despair and now has become God's vessel that carries living water!

False Burden Bearing

Our true identity, the core of our being is found within the image of God. That identity can become covered over with layers of lies which enter our souls through unresolved issues resulting from the unhealed hurts and unmet needs. We carry the burden of these lies and unhealed places to the point that we are walking through life bent over. We are shuffling along, surviving. Jesus says,

> *Take my yoke upon you… for my yoke is easy and my burden is light,*
> (Matthew 11:29-30).

Instead of seeing ourselves as victors, our identity becomes that as victim. We are bent over because we are carrying our own burdens as well as the burdens of others. This is called false burden bearing.

> *Now he was teaching in one of the synagogues on the Sabbath. And behold, there was a woman who had had a disabling spirit for eighteen years. She was bent over and could not fully straighten herself. When Jesus saw her, he called her over and said to her, "Woman, you are freed from your disability. And he laid his hands on her, and immediately she was made straight, and she glorified God.*
>
> Luke 13:10-13

What was the condition of the bent over woman?

- She had a disabling spirit for eighteen years. She was bent over. She could not straighten herself out.
- She was in the synagogue on the Sabbath where Jesus was teaching

Her disabling spirit was an infirmity of the body and/or of the soul. It can be understood both ways. Our souls can be bent over in *'need-love'* either to God or to others. To have a disabling spirit entails a loss of strength and capacity. The bent over woman had this infirmity for eighteen years signifying how difficult life was for her.

Picture being bent over. Try it yourself. See how it is to walk. What do you see while you are walking in this condition? You see only the ground in front of you. You see no farther than the next step. Even when people talk to you, you cannot raise up to encounter them or see their face. You are bowed over. The same is true for the bent over soul, bearing burdens and trials alone. This woman could not straighten herself up or out. I am sure she tried like many of us do. I used to have shelves of self-help books that only helped finance those authors! Look at her presenting identity. She is named in the New Testament as the *bent over woman*

(Luke 13:11). She has no other name and no other identity given. Her identity is her infirmity.

So, she comes to the synagogue. How she slips in without being noticed is a God-wonder in itself. But she is in the synagogue on the Sabbath and Jesus is teaching. During Jesus' time women were not allowed in the synagogue with men who were listening to the Torah or teachings. In fact *one was not so much as to greet a woman* (Talmud Berakhoth, 2010, 43b). Yet, her desire for healing was greater than her fear of man. She is at the end of her rope. Infirmities of the body or the soul can drain us emotionally and physically. Struggling daily to survive, only seeing the ground and stones in front of you strips your hope of ever thriving. The scripture does not tell us what burdens she carries but I know sometimes we even take on others' burdens that are not ours to carry, resulting in our own '*bent*' soul.

I know this bent over woman. Maybe you do too. One early morning before dawn when all was quiet, I went out to my lanai with coffee and iPad in hand. Benny, my ever-faithful rescue dog padded behind me jumping up on his spot on the sofa. I sat before the Lord just listening to the sounds of nature pre-dawn intermingled with Benny's soft snoring sounds. All was peaceful but not really. I am worried…concerned about my son. It is a difficult time in his life and I can't fix it. I couldn't even say anything to him. I could pray. And as I began to pray for him the old self-accusations of long ago began to creep back into my mind and heart: *It's your fault…you weren't there enough for him…his father left when he was young…you weren't enough for your son.* My heart begins to break…once again.

God had healed me of false-burden bearing many years ago but here it is knocking at the door of my heart again– no actually pounding at the door of my heart! I didn't recognize it at first, this familiar spirit trying to attack me by tempting me to self-denigration because of my son's present situation. The pain seared my heart like a red hot knife cutting through it. Suddenly God showed me a picture. Right in the middle of this searing heart pain, He showed me a picture of an old woman bent over. I know her! Lord I have preached her story many times.

"Look closely," I hear Him whisper. "She has your face!" Yes, she does! God has my attention! And on her back she is carrying a heavy load. I see she is bowed down so low to the ground. "Look closer," He whispers again. The load was my almost six foot tall son! I am shocked and then suddenly I begin to laugh and laugh! I couldn't carry him! The picture was ridiculous! I could carry him as a baby yes but not as a grown man! In fact, I was so bent over I was laid out flat on the ground under his weight. The comical picture of me attempting to carry this ex-football player on my back was actually hysterical! It is a picture I will never forget!

I cried out: "Jesus forgive me for trying to do your job." His words of life came pouring into my hurting heart: *Come all you who are heavy laden and I will give you rest. Take my burden upon you for my burden is light.* (Matthew 11:28-30). If the burden you are carrying is heavy, then you are not carrying what Jesus has given you to carry but are trying to carry what only He can carry.

Yes, God healed me of the spirit of false burden bearing years ago but Satan will always wait for an opportune time to strike again. The temptation was there to immerse myself in that negative behavior of carrying burdens that weren't mine to carry. Once again I was believing the old lies: *It's your fault...You weren't enough.* The key to closing the door in these temptations is honesty with God, confession, repentance, healing the root and staying in His presence. My identity is not in old failures, real or perceived but in the present new creation Jesus continues to form in me daily. Every temptation to go back to old negative behavior, is conquered by going through the painful situation now with Jesus who heals us. Now we are made stronger to face the next trial and temptation.

Think back to the old bent over woman. What is the process of healing she went through? The first thing that happens is that Jesus sees her. That is a healing in itself. Some women think they are invisible because that's how they were treated as children. The bent over woman stood out in the crowd being the only woman there. He called her over, *Woman*. It wasn't a whisper but right out loud in front of everyone. Can you imagine what she went through hearing Jesus call her? Fear! She wasn't supposed to be in the synagogue in the first place. Women weren't allowed. She had risked her life coming here. She couldn't even see Him but now He had called her out. And she heard Him. Those who had not seen her before now did! How great the tension in that place must have been! And here is the teacher, rabbi, talking to a woman publicly in a synagogue.

> *When Jesus saw her, he called her over and said to her, 'Woman, you are freed from your disability.'*
>
> (Luke 13:13).

He called her '*woman*', not bent over woman. She is not invisible to Him nor is she a victim. He declares *you are freed*. You are freed means your bonds are loosed. Liberty has been granted to you right now. Yet as all look at her, they could see she was still bent over. Jesus spoke the healing, but it hadn't manifested physically. How difficult to wait for that healing to manifest. All eyes are on her and Jesus. She shuffles her way up to Jesus, one painful step after another, her eyes cast down on the floor. Her back so horribly bent. What were the others thinking to themselves? Finally standing in front of Him still severely bent over, Jesus lays His hands on her and the healing that was spoken is now activated in her! Every cell in her body responds to the command of Jesus. Immediately she is made straight and she glorifies God right there in front of everyone! Her identity is no longer the bent over woman. She is the straightened, upright woman who glorifies God! Her true identity was there all along but the lies of the enemy had covered it over. You are not your suffering…you are not your wounds…you are not your infirmity. You are God's child.

The problem of the bent over woman is identified in Scripture. The root of the woman's bent shape, is defined as bondage. The root of our bent shapes are our bondages. If the root is not healed or straightened out, then our identity is found in these bondages, in this bentness, rather than in God. If a young boy is told during his formative years that he will not amount to anything that becomes a curse or bondage upon him the rest of his life, until it is brought to Jesus. His whole demeanor and his behaviors will be bent toward that identity rather than the one God has for him. Others will label him the same as well. This is an example of a false identity being formed by lies and curses. His true identity in God is buried beneath the lies and the word curses of the enemy that come through unhealed wounds in the boy, God says:

> *For I know the plans I have for you, declares the Lord, plans to prosper you and not to harm you, plans to give you hope and a future.*
> (Jeremiah 29:11)

Perfectionism

A dear woman I knew was struggling with perfectionism. She had to have everything perfect even to the point that her compulsive behavior began to take hold of her every day activities. For example, she could not take one tissue out of a box, it had to be two. Fairness was mixed up with perfection. She had to have things in order and not out of alignment. This was wearing on her and her family. Her identity was wrapped up in all this thought: *I have to be perfect.* With her permission, here is her account of this bondage of perfectionism, a block to her true identity in Christ, and how God healed her:

I was sick and tired of dealing with this need to be perfect, to do everything just right. I was tired of always being the one in a meeting or a personal interaction who wasn't able to pause and have fun, always wanting to get on with whatever was the task at hand. So I took this to the Lord one morning in prayer and asked Him to help me see the root issue for this need to do things perfectly. The Lord immediately gave me the remembrance of a photograph of myself as a child. I went and found the photo in a box in my closet. It was me at 3 years old. I was leaning across the kitchen table, looking at the camera, grinning from ear to ear, and there was a birthday cake in front of me with three candles on it.

I took this picture to a healing prayer team and told them that it was the only clue the Lord had given me when I asked him for the root of my perfectionism. We prayed and I asked the Lord, "When did I quit being so carefree like I was in the picture?" Immediately a memory of me at 5 years old surfaced. It was a time I had remembered as an adult and had laughed at what had happened as "the day I almost drowned my brother". It was the day my brand new baby brother was brought home from the hospital and he was lying in the basinet. He had the hiccups and I went and got him a glass of water to help him.

Everyone in the room stopped me with "No don't!" No one was mad but they just stopped me because he was too small for a glass of water.

God showed me that as the five-year-old, I felt confusion and embarrassment because I just wanted to be a good big sister. I didn't know what I had done was wrong. (I feel sure someone explained it to me, but God had me focused on that initial moment of confusion). And as loud as I have ever heard my heart speak, I heard my five-year-old self inside exclaim: "I will never make another mistake again". And there was an inner vow of perfectionism made at 5 years old. From that point on my identity was bent toward perfectionism, my bondage. Every job I took became perfection and performance oriented. If I made a mistake I was devastated. In the healing prayer time, I had the sense of Jesus being there with me, wanting to comfort me but my arms were folded tight and I was adamantly saying those words. "I will never make another mistake again!" I was 44 years old when I did this prayer... 39 years of bondage to that vow!

Jesus and I, with support of my healing prayer partners, broke the power of that vow in His Name and authority. I asked His forgiveness for ever putting that kind of bondage on my life. For accepting it so easily! Suddenly I felt so free and relieved. To have permission in my heart to be able to make a mistake and not be angry with myself was an amazing feeling. The guilt was gone!

Two years later, God did another piece of this healing with me. It was Thursday, the last bit of preparation going on for the Healing conference that would start that night. 150 people were signed up to come and I was the administrator in charge of the conference. One of the volunteers came to me with a problem. All the holes had been punched on the wrong side of the pages of one chapter outline of the healing curriculum and there was no time to fix them for the conference the way I wanted them to be fixed. All we could do was go back thru all the books and punch holes on the right side of the pages, thus having holes on both sides of the page. Everything in me was struggling with this. It made "my teeth hurt". We stopped and prayed right then and Jesus took me to a creative prayer where he and the youth were in the conference playfully looking at each other through the holes in the pages. And in a moment, Jesus turned face-on to me and looked at me through those same holes and said, "I look past your mistakes at you." I began to weep, fell to the floor, and all the shame came off of me. I WAS NOT MY MISTAKES! Jesus finished the good work He had begun - first the guilt two years before and then the shame. "What freedom! Amen!"

False Identity

True identity is being yourself and being yourself means you know you are a child of God. Our true identity as children of God can be compromised or covered over by past wounds and hurts that have not been healed. As a result one can take on a false identity, which is when someone pretends to be someone they aren't and can never be. Often a person loses one's identity trying to please or placate other people. Some people grew up in homes where they weren't recognized or were told to be silent, their opinions not worthwhile.

An attractive woman walked into my office one day. She felt she just couldn't seem to move forward in her profession. We had never met before and after a few moments of pleasantries, she lowered her head and said she wasn't feeling good about herself. I asked Holy Spirit to take her to the root of this block in her profession and the negative feelings she was having about herself. She saw herself as a seven year old little girl, down on her knees scrubbing the old tile floors in her family's house. Quickly she explained that she and her older brother were adopted – coming from different parents. In the memory that God brought to her she saw people walking back and forth and not even noticing she was there scrubbing the floor! She was quite upset – she saw herself as a slave to be used for labor but not to be heard or really seen. She felt invisible. "Invisible, yes that's what I am," she said.

She asked Jesus to show Himself to her as this confession of being invisible tore at her heart. "He's here! He is right alongside of me! Why He's helping me!" Apparently she was not invisible to God. She immediately felt better. She was shocked as she, the adult, looked at her little seven year. old self there with Jesus, I asked her if she liked that little girl. "No, I don't," she responded. The little girl within her tried to speak but couldn't – she had been silenced for a long time not just by the adults in the house but by her adult self as well. She too had rejected the little girl living within her. Suddenly she saw her little girl inside her in terrible pain. Her inner child was so wounded! Her own adult tears began to flow first from her adult self but then from the wounded little girl inside of her. As her adult heart melted, she said, "I want to hug this little one!" Coming closer and with Jesus standing there she did hug that little one. Tears flowed both from her adult self and her little girl self, for finally they could weep together after all the years of feeling invisible and rejected. Jesus held them both. As the adult she asked the little one to forgive her for the judgment she had placed on her and for rejecting her. Forgiveness was immediate. Forgiving her parents came haltingly at first but then freely. Suddenly she exclaimed, "Oh my! Oh my! Jesus just put my little girl-self and my adult-self together! I am whole for the first time in my life! And I am visible... wonderfully wholly visible!" This is the first reconciliation that had to take place before she could reconcile with anyone else in her life. And what a reconciliation!

Do you have a false identity? Are you:

- Trying too hard to please others
- Pretending to be what you are not; like wearing a mask
- Feeling lonely and disconnected – like an orphan spirit
- Feeling lost and not sure how to act in situations
- Feeling depressed and helpless with no hope
- Afraid of making mistakes and being rejected
- Fearful of relationships that require commitment
- Not using the gifts God has placed in you.
- Not free to be yourself in the Body of Christ
- Experiencing confusion

Answering yes to any of these questions points out that somewhere within, you are harboring a false identity that has roots in your past. These roots negatively affects your present behavior and thoughts about yourself and others.

To help you get to the core of your identity you can ask yourself a different question: Who aren't you? God contradicts all the false identities that the world and Satan try to put on you. The false identities spoken into you by the evil one as a result of deep wounding are countered and demolished by Gods Word. His truth about who you are is affirmed through the Holy Spirit in inner healing encounters with God.

- You are not your past. (*Therefore, if anyone is in Christ, the new creation has come: the old has gone, the new is here!* 2 Corinthians 5:17)
- You are not what you own. (*He who loves money will not be satisfied with money, he who loves wealth with his income; this also was vanity.* Ecclesiastes 5:10)
- You are not what others think of you (*The spiritual person judges all things, but is himself to be judged by no one.* 1 Corinthians 2:15)
- You are not the way you look. (*Do not judge by appearances, but judge with right judgment.* John 7:24)
- You are not the feelings you have. (*The heart is deceitful above all things, and desperately sick; who can understand it?* Jeremiah 17:9)
- You are not your successes nor your failures. (*My flesh and my heart may fail, but God is the strength of my heart and my portion forever.* Psalm 73:26)

The Pharisee and the Imposter

Brennen Manning (1994) in his book *Abbas Child* names two false identities: *The Pharisee and the Imposter*:

> *Two men went up into the temple to pray, one a Pharisee and the other a tax collector.*
>
> (Luke 18:10)

A Pharisee carries religion like a shield of self-justification and a sword of judgment. Remember Paul was once identified as a Pharisee who ravaged the church, (Acts 8:1-3; 9:1-2).

Pharisees exhibit rule ridden perfectionism. "They falsify the image of God into an eternal small minded bookkeeper whose favor can only be won by scrupulous observance of laws and regulations," (Manning, 1994). The resulting legalistic religion intimidates a congregation and keeps them bound. Pharisaism is reflected in the laws of our early American history.

Code of Connecticut:

> *No one shall run on the Sabbath Day or walk in his garden or elsewhere except reverently to and from meeting. No one shall travel, cook victuals, make beds, sweep house, cut hair or shave on the Sabbath. If any man shall kiss his wife or wife her husband on the Lord's Day, the party in fault shall be punished at the discretion of the court magistrates.* (Manning, 1994, p 80)

People were afraid to be honest about their thoughts and behavior in public and so they pretended to be extremely moral. This toxic atmosphere of pseudo-piety encouraged hiddenness. Our early churches were making disciples that were judgmental, robot-like in worship, and intolerant of others and themselves. Pharisees are blamers, accusers, and love to lay guilt on others. *Everything they do is for show. On their arms they wear extra-wide prayer boxes with scripture verses inside, and they were gross with extra-long tassels.* (Matthew 23:5, New Living Translation). The Pharisee sees the speck in another's eye but not the plank in his own. Even now while reading this you can think of many people who fit this description of a Pharisee, but hold on…we have to look back at ourselves.

The theology of the Pharisee is a theology of works. The children in their families must earn love. There is no room for mistakes. Doing everything right is the expectation. Children in these families do not express negative feelings or needs. They feel they have to earn love.

The theology of works can be found in churches all over the world. My team and I flew from Santa Cruz, Bolivia, to Sucre, the capital of Bolivia. From there we took a van along narrow mountainous roads gratefully arriving in Potosi, which is situated 14,000 feet above sea level. Looking down over the precipitous cliffs while driving even ones gasps of fear were measured by the thinness of the air! We had been invited by the Bishop of the Church of God to minister to several churches along the way. This particular church was led by a Bolivian couple with the wife as the pastor of the church, a very powerful preacher. I stood looking out over the crowd that had jammed into that little church with many standing outside and my heart melted with God's love for them because of the hunger the people had for God. There is freedom here to worship and cry out to God. There is expectation and understanding that God is present and is with you no matter how difficult the circumstances are in your life. All this in the midst of much poverty and difficult living conditions.

Though I did not perceive this church to be carrying a Pharisaic spirit at all, I was led by the Holy Spirit to preach that night on the unconditional love of God My focus was that no one could earn His love for God gives it freely to all who call on His name. I asked, "How many of you feel like you have to earn love?" And many hands went up including Ileana, the female pastor. This surprised me. As I preached on God's love, His love began to descend on them like a warm blanket. His love was so palpable! Soft weeping began as God's love melted their hearts. The team spread out and began praying with the people to heal the roots of the devil's lie *'You have to earn love'*. God's truth, *Freely, freely you have received...* replaced the enemy's lie. Prayers poured out for healing in each one's life. Loud weeping erupted! The Holy Spirit was ministering everywhere even out the doors of the church onto the street. The Pharisaic spirit which I had not seen at first was exposed and had to flee because the love of God always prevails and endures forever. The truth set each one free! Oh what a celebration ensued!

Pastor Ileana needed inner healing that night too but she was more concerned about her church, so she did not receive it specifically for herself. The next few days after ministering at a church in Sucre I became very ill. The evil one is never pleased when we bring the love of God into a place and confront the enemy, in this case, the Pharisaic spirit that was dominating in that geographical area. It is no contest because that battle has been won at the cross by the shed blood and resurrection of Jesus Christ and now is won in people's souls as we minister that love in Christ's Name. So, Satan will attack the messengers of God's light always trying to intimidate and stop them. He is really trying to kill Jesus in us which is a lost cause!

Turning more ashen by the minute, the illness was ravaging my body. With tickets to fly out that day to Cochabamba to lead a women's healing conference in two days, we prayed and prayed. I remained very ill. By God's grace heavy cloud cover prevented us from flying that day. It cleared the next day and we flew out. Everyone was praying for me! I laid in the back of the plane across three seats. By the grace of God I made it but I looked, as my southern grandmother would say, like 'death warmed over!' I felt that way too. And here I was, coming to lead and preach on the healing of God! One of the pastor's wives who happened to be a doctor came and brought me some medication and the healing prayers continued. After a night-long battle with this physical attack, complete with fever and chills and all the other misery that comes with an intestinal illness, the battle was done and won! I got up the next morning, feeling renewed, energized, and full color was back in my face. Arriving at the breakfast table I said "I'm hungry!" as the team stared at me in disbelief! I did not look like I had even been sick! Our God is an awesome God!

The women's conference began and again that Pharisaic spirit became evident. The women were not free to fully worship. I could see the pain and suffering etched on their faces and the hunger for God evident in their tears. The Holy Spirit let me see that the women had little regard for themselves...they were beaten down...invisible...victims. I could see in the spirit realm the burdens they were carrying. So bowed down, it hurt the hearts of our whole team. The leadership was not holding them back but the unhealed places, unmet needs in their hearts and the lies of the enemy blocked them from fully entering into the love and freedom in God. The women came from all different parts of Bolivia. Many were given financial assistance to help get them there. At first even Pastor Ileana had no way of getting there but generous donations provided the means for her to come. I was over-joyed at seeing her again! How much God loves us!

The next day we planned on getting to the root of the Pharisaic spirit as the Holy Spirit led us. I also knew that God wanted me to anoint the female pastors after receiving their own healing so they could go and minister in His authority among the many women there. Pastor Ileana was filled with anticipation of God's healing and anointing. Suddenly she became ill and couldn't attend the Saturday sessions. During a break the women led me to her room. Her face lit up as we walked into the room and there we prayed. Nothing stops God from His work.

The Holy Spirit took her back to the time when her father died when she was nine years old. Haltingly she said, "He used to hug me but never told me he loved me." She was quiet and we waited and then she spoke, "I worked so hard for him to love me…...never felt like I pleased him… then he died." Ah, the root of the Pharisaic spirit that had been dogging her all her life.

Jesus took her to the time when her dad died. Remember, God is eternal, meaning he is outside of time and He is Lord of our past as well as our present and future. Jesus showed her the memory of her dad in the hospital room. Suddenly she saw Jesus with her dad and she knew right then and there that he was saved! Joy burst out on her face! That was the first healing. Then she saw herself as the little nine year old girl coming near the bed where her father lay. Jesus was standing next to him. Her father said, "I love you." She hugged him while weeping deep, long, pent up tears and there that little nine-year-old forgave him for not telling her before. She saw him weeping too. Cleansing tears washed through her as she released her dad to Jesus. The Pharisaic spirit was exposed and the truth of God's love drove that spirit out and healed her broken heart! She was also healed physically and able to join the rest of the conference!

Remember the theology of a Pharisee is a theology of works. Pharisees set themselves apart. They follow the law to the letter in order to induce God's love. This is the child who does everything right, never pouts, cries, whines, does all her chores, etc. This is the child who shares no negative feelings, never expresses needs.....all to earn love. The Pharisee usurps his real self whenever he prefers appearances to reality.

How do we get healed of the Pharisaic spirit? First, we have to acknowledge the spirit within. But that is not as easy as it sounds. We must get to the root of this spirit in order to be healed of it. Actually, the Pharisaic spirit operating within a person is really the face of an imposter. Brennen Masnning states that this idealistic, perfectionist and neurotic self is oppressed by a *terrorist spirituality*. This is so interesting. Terrorists are bullies who attempt to intimidate by fear. We know about terrorists in our society today. Terrorists demand submission. Terrorists are bullies and where there is a Pharisaic spirit there is a bully operating within us. The bully within us is also called a persecutor, oppressor, tyrant, accuser, tormentor and intimidator. What does this inner bully inside us say?

- What an idiot I am!
- Stay back, I can't take a risk
- Who do I think I am that God will hear me? Or heal me? Or use me?
- I'm worthless.
- God won't forgive me....
- There's too many other hurting people...I can't break through....

Researchers estimate we have on average 70,000 thoughts in the course of a single day. Now some of those thoughts are going to be negative but when our negative thoughts outweigh our positive ones we have a problem.

As you are reading this section write done your negative thoughts. Do it right now, expose them. Ask the Holy Spirit to bring them to the surface. For the Truth will set you free. The Holy Spirit will show you the origin of these negative thoughts. Go to that root and let Jesus heal that negative thought hiding there. As you forgive others and yourself, God will speak the Truth into you setting you free. This is to take captive every thought and defeat the bully within you. If a thought puts you down, then it does not glorify God nor even acknowledge Him. Why? Because you are made in God's image and that means you are fearfully and wonderfully made (Psalm 139).

Our strong desire for security is the compulsion that drives a work-oriented way of living. We want to feel safe. That's why legalism or Pharisaism is so attractive. The rules and the regulations give us a false security. This encourages the drive for perfection in everything. A person's compulsion to feel safe with God fuels this desire for perfection. They feel they have to earn this security. Of course, the opposite happens. Trying to earn God's love and security, blocks feeling accepted by God. This leads to feelings of failure which leads to lowered self-esteem which triggers anxiety, fear, depression, even panic attacks. What a vicious cycle!

At the bottom of this compulsion for perfection, as seen in Pharisaic behavior, lies the Imposter. The Imposter is the false self that lives within us. What are the characteristics of the false self?

- The imposter lives in fear.
- The imposter is preoccupied with acceptance and approval.
- The imposter demands to be noticed.

- The imposter also draws his identity from interpersonal relationships.
- The imposter can't experience intimacy in any relationship. Reciprocal sharing is impossible.

The imposter is born when we as children were not loved well or were rejected or abandoned. The imposter is defined by what he does! Reality is too painful and so it is distorted, thus compromising truth.

If we claim to be without sin, we deceive ourselves and the truth is not in us.

(I John 1:8 NIV)

The Imposter does not live an abundant life but settles for a diminished life. The Imposter operates out of a fear-based center not a love-based center. *Perfect love casts out fear* (1 John 4:18). Negative memories and/or repressed memories are too painful to recall and deal with openly. They remain buried and self-deception is now the pattern set in this person's life. Avoidance of feeling rejection at all costs is another driver.

The Imposter within also interacts with God this way. They can be super-religious, super busy Christians, as a way to avoid intimacy with God and with others. Craving mood altering experiences, hungering for spiritual highs, for some becomes their spiritual modus operandi.

There can only be two basic loves, the love of God unto the forgetfulness of self or the love of self unto the forgetfulness of God. St Augustine of Hippo (St. Augustine R. C. Church, 2019)

The root of the imposter is traced back to Adam and Eve.

And they heard the sound of the Lord God walking in the garden in the cool of the day, and Adam and his wife hid themselves from the presence of the Lord God among the trees of the garden.
(Genesis 3:8 NKJV)

Adam and Eve hid. The imposter hides from God and from their true self. If they had hidden themselves in God perhaps things might have been different. We have that opportunity now. When we sin or the enemy is after us, we can hide in God under the shadow of His wings.

Rescue me from my enemies, O Lord, for I hide myself in you.
(Psalm 143:9)

The Hebrew word for hide (kacah, '*kaw-saw*') at its root means as to fill up hollows in us. By implication, to cover us either with God's righteous garments or garments of secrecy. Secrets keep us sick and in shame. How do we heal the imposter within?

God asked, "Where are you Adam?" The imposter must be called out from hiding, accepted and embraced by one's own self. Denial is a huge stronghold and prevents us from being whole and real. Whatever is denied cannot be healed. The false self must be dismantled. We all have a shadow side. Psychology states that this may be the least desirable aspects of our personality that we reject or choose to remain ignorant about. Scripture states that once we were darkness (shadows) but now we are light. (Ephesians 5:8). This is a description of the shadow side of us being healed. Remember the scripture where Peter's shadow healed people? (Acts 5:15). This would indicate the healing of his shadow!

> *Even the darkness is not dark to you; the night is bright as the day, for darkness is as light to you,*
>
> **(Psalm 139:12).**

Another interesting insight is that God, who makes good out of everything Satan means for evil, uses Peter's shadow to heal others.

Peace lies in the acceptance of God's truth. We all have a wounded shadow self and every part of ourselves, all our brokenness, must be exposed and embraced in order to be healed. What we will not expose, accept, and embrace becomes our enemy (the enemy *'inna me'*). Henri Nouwen writes:

> *How can we respond to brokenness? There are two ways: first, the befriending it and second, putting it under the blessing. The first response then is to face it squarely and befriend it. My own pain in life has taught me that the first step to healing is not a step away from the pain but a step toward it. Brokenness is just as much a part of us as our chosenness and our blessedness. We live our brokenness either under the curse or under the blessing. Living it under the curse means that we experience our pain as a confirmation of our negative feelings about ourselves. It's like saying 'I always suspected that I was useless or worthless now I'm sure of it because of what's happening to me.' The great call of God to his beloved children is to pull their brokenness away from the shadow of the curse and put it under the light of the blessing (2002)*

Healing of the imposter within us occurs as the Light of Christ shines into the unhealed darkness within, exposing the lies of the enemy and healing the deep wounds of rejection. Several people in the bible did not allow their shadow side to be healed. The rich young ruler is one who actually hung onto his shadowy side. Judas who betrayed Jesus would not embrace his shadow side. He never sought God for forgiveness and he self-destructed.

Who did allow God to heal their shadow side? Peter certainly did as evidenced by Jesus reinstating him at the end of the Gospel of John. The Samaritan woman at the well who did not deny her past but instead allowed Jesus to expose it, then received His love, which transformed her life. Mary Magdalene who was delivered of many demons, allowed every part of herself to be exposed to Jesus, even her unbelief concerning His resurrection from the dead. Yet in all her frailty as a human being, in all her doubts and deep grieving, she still sought Jesus even if it was among the dead. The Imposter had no chance with her. It didn't matter how bad things looked, she still sought Jesus. And she found Him for He was there all along!

It's critical we come to grips with the Imposter within ourselves if the imposter is going to be cast out and our soul healed.

> *Embrace the imposter... accept that we are impoverished and broken.... we are not God. If we are accepting with ourselves we will be with others. i.e. gentle with ourselves then gentle with others.* (Henri Nouen, 2002)

If we don't embrace the imposter within, the enemy will use our brokenness, our shadow side, against ourselves and others. The deceiver will first deceive us and then we will put on a false appearance and deceive others.

During a particularly hard time in my ministry during my seventh year as rector of a church I faced this Imposter within myself. God gave me the opportunity to do this though I didn't quite see it that way at first. As a result of over working and taking on more than God ever asked me to, I found myself physically and emotionally spent. I had burned all the ends of candles there were to burn! My church leadership, my bishop and I, though begrudgingly on my part, agreed that I would take an overdue sabbatical to regain my strength physically, emotionally, and spiritually. Right about this time someone sent me a book by John

Sanford (1992) titled *Ministry Burn Out*. That's what was going on with me! I had not even heard of that before but as I read his painful account of going through burnout, I wept. That sabbatical lasted four months. During that time, rumors abounded with all kinds of reasons I was no longer at the church. By the grace of God, I had come out of alcoholism in 1983, and by His grace continued in sobriety. That was one of the ugly rumors that abounded, that I had relapsed with alcohol. I told the clergy person who called me to inform me of that rumor, "I hope I had a good time!"

But I had relapsed not with alcoholism but in judgement…in over work…in striving. Somehow God had been moved off to the side and ministry had become the top priority. I lost my first love. After the initial shock wore off that I was not going into the office daily nor preaching every Sunday as I had for seven years, I began to experience anger. I had always downplayed my anger, after all as the daughter of a southern woman, I knew that southern women don't get angry. Oh but how wrong I was for I was angry! How could this have happened to me? Our church was so alive and growing and the healing ministry had taken off. We had grown from twenty-five to one hundred eighty on-fire members. Our healing ministry conferences had attendance in the hundreds with so many lives changed. How could this have happened to our church? To me? Why didn't the leaders prevent it? And where were they now? My anger was placed towards others. I felt extremely alone. My heart was wrenched in pain. Nagging me deep within was the irony that I was a leader in the healing ministry and I was a mess!

I sought help from a Christian therapist, a healing contemplative priest, a Bishop, a few old friends and my family, but most of all God. My own bishop called me every week to see how I was doing which meant a great deal to me, but still the anger I didn't want to acknowledge seethed inside me. The deep wound of rejection from so long ago in my childhood, surfaced again. I couldn't ignore this. Inside it felt like a storm brewing, tossing me about, and pitting my own emotions against me. Sensing a darkness in me that I hated and didn't want, I pushed it further down. The harder I fought it, the stronger this darkness became. One particularly hard day while sitting out on my lanai in tears and anguish, this overwhelming rage surfaced. Hot molten anger like lava bursting out of a pent-up volcano erupted! The pain was searing. The anger was all aimed at the church leaders. Throwing myself onto the tile floor I screamed out, "Let their little ones be dashed against the rocks," (Psalm 137:9). Suddenly in horror, in sheer horror, I saw the blackness of my own heart. It was abominable! I had no idea such venom could be living in me. The shadow side now exposed, erupted out of control. The hot lava of the long ago rejection by the man who fathered me, who was supposed to love me and care for me, mixed now with other hurtful rejections along the way, poured out of me. Weeping and yelling and sobbing, finally after many hours I lay spent on the floor. No more tears left, no more anger to expend. The imposter in me had been exposed and had no place to live in me anymore. This is where the healing began in me.

God's sacred child, me, had been torn in two by the ravages of my own brokenness; a brokenness I had not been willing to embrace before at its deepest roots. After all God had brought me through so many broken places in my life. I told people I was a poster child for the broken! Look what God can do with broken pieces. Yet, the shadow-self lurked beneath all this healing that had transpired in my life, knowing I had not dealt with the Imposter within that covered up the orphan child.

An orphan child is one who has been abandoned by a parent. One can have an orphan spirit even if parents have not physically abandoned that child. This person with an orphan spirit has a sense of abandonment, loneliness, alienation and rejection. Breaking and healing the orphan spirit occurs when one is filled with the Father's love for them in Christ. The truth is that we are all adopted sons and daughters of our heavenly Father. The truth is that there are no orphans in God's kingdom!

Here on a cold tile floor God met me at my lowest, most broken and blackest point and here began to heal, reconcile, and resurrect my torn soul. Here I embraced my humanity with all its scars, open wounds, and just plain messiness. Only now could I begin to embrace my God-given divinity, *Christ in me, the hope of glory!* I am a child of God! I am His daughter!

Tenth Avenue North sings a poignant song summing up my encounter with the imposter within. The title of the song is: *This Is Where the Healing Begins.*

"All the work that you do..."

So let it fall down.... (Ingram, Owen, Donehey, 2010)

Summation

Healing our identity is about soul-making. Conversion is the process of being made and re-made in our soul. The false self must be dismantled so Christ's mantle can be placed on us. We really put on Christ! When we accept Christ as our Lord and Savior and give Him our hearts, this is just the beginning of our healing and transformation. There is a need now to put in right order our personality and character. When we experienced our conversion it didn't mean that our soul followed along necessarily! We still have unhealed hurts, unmet needs and unresolved issues that must be exposed and healed. We still have wounds and faulty belief systems that must be exposed and healed. We still have habitual negative behaviors that resulted from these unhealed places in our lives to correct and transform. If these areas are not healed we become Christians who wound others in the midst of doing ministry. Suppose we are judgmental and this is not repented of, healed and covered in God's love, then we will judge others without mercy believing we are right. We do not want to fulfill the premise that wounded people wound others.

Then he will answer them, saying, 'Assuredly, I say to you, inasmuch as you did not do it to one of the least of these, you did not do it to Me.'
(Matthew 25:45 NKJV).

Who are the least? We are the least!!! We have met the least and the least is us! Jesus saves us from ourselves and heals us to reveal the true self within each of us – and that true self is made in His image.

For in Christ the whole fullness of deity dwells bodily and you have been filled in him who is the head of all rule and authority.
(Colossians 2:9-10 ESV)

Chapter 5
BLOCKS TO HEALING: INNER VOWS, WORD CURSES, LIES OF THE ENEMY, GENERATIONAL SIN

Inner vows, word curses, lies of the enemy, sexual and soul ties, and generational sin are blocks to healing in our soul.

Inner Vows

I will not be an alcoholic like my biological father. That is the inner vow I made about my biological father. It sounds good, moral, even ethical! It is nevertheless a judgment on a parent and those types of judgments will come back on us. The very thing I vowed, I became! Why? I judged my father.

God commands that we honor our fathers and mothers that our days may be long with us.

> *Honor your father and your mother, so that you may live long in the land the Lord your God is giving you.*
>
> Exodus 20:12

We are not to judge their character or motivations, though we may judge their behavior. God has placed mothers and fathers in a position of authority. We still must honor that commandment of God, regardless of circumstances. If you were abused that action or abuse is never acceptable, but we must still honor the position that God placed upon parents by not judging their character or motivations. Easy? Absolutely not! Only God can do this in us through and with His love. God will do the judging.

What is an inner vow? An inner vow is a determination set by the mind and heart into our being usually in the early years of life. At a young age we make these vows to try and gain control of a situation. These inner vows are set in us when we are children as decisions and directives. They are usually forgotten. The way children interpret painful, traumatic, hurtful, even disciplinary action results in the formation of these inner vows, and they remain on the hard drive of our souls no matter what changes happen in life.

Inner vows resist change. You do not grow out of them; they continue to be underlying drivers of our behaviors today. Initially these inner wows served as protectors from the unsafe situations or hurtful events in our childhood. For example, as I prayed with one young woman she said, "I have to do everything." As we prayed, the root of this inner vow came as she was told by her chronically ill mother that she had to be in charge of the house at age eleven. She carried that inner vow into her adult life and was now angry that no one helped her with all the responsibilities of raising two young children and taking care of a home while working.

It is important to note that we all have made inner vows in our lives. These inner vows are powerful and many continue to operate today in our lives, though they are difficult to identify.

How can you spot an inner vow? Inner vows often begin with, I will never..., or I will always... We are making determinations about our lives that are not ours to make. In addition we are putting judgments on others at the time we make the inner vow.

For example:

- *I will never be like my dad (or mom).*
- *I will always take care of myself.*
- *I will never grow up.*
- *I'll always be a failure, no matter how hard I try.*
- *I'll always do something to mess things up!*
- *I'll never let anyone get close again.*
- *I always have to do everything myself*
- *I will always do things perfectly.*

Biblical principles instruct us not to judge. We reap what we sow.

> *Do not be deceived: God cannot be mocked. A man reaps what he sows. What you sow you will reap.*
>
> **Galatians 6:7**

It is only by God's grace that we have the power not to fall prey to our own judgments. Even the words spoken with good intentions, will backfire at times. A young man told me, "I will never be angry and hit my spouse like my parent did." Yet he still judges his parent. Only God is allowed to judge. We all get angry but we do not have to act on it like our parent(s) did. If violence was part of your growing up, it is critical you receive healing for the violent events that happened in your childhood, so you do not carry on that destructive behavior generation to generation. This can be eradicated and healed through your generations through Jesus Christ by the power of the Holy Spirt. God will do the judging of the character of the ones who were the abusers.

> *Do not judge, or you too will be judged? For in the same way you judge others, you will be judged, and with the measure you use, it will be measured to you. 'Why do you look at the speck of sawdust in your brother's eye and pay no attention to the plank in your own eye?*
>
> (Matthew 7:1-3)

Inner vows are not only a judging problem but also demonstrations of us relying on our own human power and strength to accomplish it. We are not relying on God to accomplish His will and thereby we open the door for Satan to attack our souls. That inner vow will work backwards or in reverse and become a word curse on ourselves, like mine did with alcoholism.

A friend recently said this vow, "I always get upset, sick and depressed this time of year when the anniversary of my mother's death rolls around." And yes she did! The vow was a self-fulfilling prophecy. She became so upset, sick and depressed at that time of year that it affected her soul and physical body.

While we do not grow out of these inner vows, we can break them off of our lives today through Jesus Christ by the power of the Holy Spirit.

Steps for breaking an inner vow:

1. Ask the Holy Spirit to reveal an inner vow that you have made. You may already have discovered one while reading this chapter. Give the Holy Spirit time to do this with you.
2. Say the inner vow out loud.
3. Ask the Holy Spirit to take you to the time in your life when you made this inner vow. You may remember a particular event in your childhood or you may see a picture or have a feeling that is uncomfortable. Jesus states I am with you always and Scripture affirms that He is the same yesterday, today and forever. Let Him show Himself to you in this event or picture or feeling. He is already there. You may experience His peace, or see Him directly

or feel warmth or see light, however God wants to show Himself to you. God wants you to know that He is with you now as He was then. He is outside of time.
4. With God's perspective on the situation, you will have an understanding of why you made the vow, and desire to give control of your life back to Him. Repent for the vow you made. If another person hurt you, Jesus will help you repent of the judgment you made on the person who hurt you.
5. Next forgive the one who harmed you. You are not condoning their behavior but you are releasing them from your judgment and thus releasing them to Jesus. You are setting yourself free at the same time. You are no longer held in bondage by this vow. Ask God to forgive you for taking on His job as judge.
6. Persevere: We must overcome long practiced negative habits associated with that vow. That may take time but never give up.

It is important to recognize that inner vows do not exist in a vacuum. They come about because of past hurtful experiences. The process of renouncing and healing inner vows, detailed above, is most powerful and effective when the memories and the feelings of the event associated with the inner vow are healed.

It is critical that you go to the root of the inner vow. The Holy Spirit will lead you there. You don't have to know what it is. At the root Jesus encounters you in that painful event and heals the origin of the inner vow. Tracking the fruit of a behavior to its root was discussed in Chapter 3 under Root Causes. There is nothing past about a harmful event in our childhood if it is still negatively effecting us today. This is a key concept and powerful reason for the ministry of inner healing.

Word Curses

Another block to healing is word curses. The power of a word is life and death. In Matthew's Gospel chapter 12 verses 33-39, Jesus explains good fruit comes from good trees, and bad fruit from bad trees. Out from our heart flows what is stored up inside. What we say reveals what is in our heart. What kinds of words come from your mouth?

I once had a young couple in my office for marital counseling work. In the midst of tears they revealed they both spoke vilely toward one another when in heated arguments. I asked the husband to tell me a few of the words he used.

Stammering, he said, "I can't. They are awful."

I pressed him because he had to hear what he was saying. He had a very difficult time saying those vile words in front of me. He was so ashamed. Eventually through choked whispers he said a few of those harmful words. I asked him, "If someone came into your home and spoke these words to your wife what would you do?"

He immediately responded, "I'd hit him!" Silence... awkward silence... as the reality sunk in that he was that person violating his wife.

After a pause I asked the wife to say some of the words she had spoken to her husband. Her eyes popped wide open, never thinking I would ask her to do the same thing. She could barely speak through her sobs. The awful disparaging words finally came. Word curses are devastating and continue to live once spoken within earshot of others' hearts!

However you can't solve your heart problems just by cleaning up your speech. You must allow the Holy Spirit to fill you with new attitudes and motives. We murder souls by speaking negative words. You will never amount to anything, may seem like a good tough love way to encourage a teen to produce but it will backfire instead. For in your authority as that child's parent you have placed a curse over the child of not amounting to anything. That child will struggle even more trying to be successful. Even saying you are just like your dad or your mother often are word curses.

The book *Restoring the Foundations: An Integrated Approach in Healing Ministry* by Chester and Betsy Kylstra (2001) defines a word curse. "A curse is the penalty to be paid for breaking a law. The biblical meaning is 'the consequence that will occur because of disobedience and rebellion against God's law.' A word curse is an appeal or prayer for evil or injury to befall someone or something." Kenneth Copeland states, "A curse is being 'empowered to fail.' A blessing is being 'empowered to succeed.'"

Word curses are cast or spoken in two ways: (1) A demonic or occult spirit may cast supernatural word curses, i.e. witchcraft and voodoo and (2) word curses spoken about us and/or to us or by us. Word curses can be spoken by us to ourselves. They may be about anything: finances, health, raising children, relationships, and expected outcomes. A middle-aged woman at a healing service said to me, "I'm afraid to get involved with anyone because anyone who comes close to me dies." Most of her family had died, many tragically. I recognized the generational word curse on this family.

What are the negative effects of word curses? First of all, they have no expiration date. When these curses are spoken into an unhealed soul, or a soul not fully surrendered to God, they take hold of that soul. Therefore, word curses have power and authority in that person's life. Whole generations can be bound by these word curses until they are broken through by Jesus Christ's redeeming work on the cross. They actually become the negative filter through which all of life is seen and understood unless broken.

For example, a curse of poverty is spoken over a family from generation to generation. A middle-aged man explained, "Our family always has to scratch and claw for everything. We never make it out of being poor. This is spoken every time something goes wrong financially in the family." The word curse of poverty is the filter through which life is viewed. The demonic spirit of scarcity has a foothold. Inner vows like Why try, I'll only fail or I will never succeed intermingle with the word curses. This is in direct opposition to the word of God.

And God is able to bless you abundantly, so that in all things at all times, having all you need, you will abound in every good work,
(2 Corinthians 9:8).

How do you break word curses? The process is similar to breaking an inner vow.

1. Ask the Holy Spirit to reveal the word curse that you or others have made against you. You may already have discovered one while reading this chapter. Give the Holy Spirit time to do this with you.
2. Say what you have discovered and immediately take authority over that word curse, breaking it in the Name of Jesus Christ. .
3. Ask the Holy Spirit to take you to the root of this word curse in your past. You may remember a particular event in your childhood, or you may see a picture or have a feeling that is uncomfortable. You may even remember a generational story that has been passed down from generation to generation. Maybe it is seen as something funny in the family! Remember Jesus states, I am with you always and scripture affirms that He is the same yesterday, today and forever. Let Him show Himself to you as the root of the word curse is exposed.
4. Bind yourself – your mind, will, emotions, physical body - to Christ. St Patrick's Breastplate Hymn exhorts each of us: "I bind unto myself today the strong name of the Trinity," (Hymn #172, Lutheran Worship, author, Irish, 1st published 1774). Certain Scriptures that apply to the area of the word curses in your life can be spoken aloud over you.

5. Repent and renounce the word curse you or others made over you. Repent for believing that word curse.
6. Ask God to forgive you for accepting this word curse. Forgive those who spoke that word curse over you including yourself and past generations.
7. Renounce this word curse in the Name of Jesus Christ and by the power of the Holy Spirit. Loose off in the Name of Jesus Christ any negative effects of that curse on you and/or your family.
8. Persevere, claiming victory in your life in the Name of Jesus Christ. Put on the mind of Christ daily as old thoughts may try to invade your mind and heart again. We must overcome long practiced harmful habits. Daily cast down imaginations and every high thing that exalts itself against the knowledge of God and bring into captivity every thought to the obedience of Christ, (2 Corinthians 10:5).

There may be more inner healing needed in the area of word curses. More may be discovered as you proceed on this healing journey with the Lord. Again, pray through each discovered word curse, being led by the Holy Spirit to the root of each one. Memories are attached many times to the origins of these word curses. The unhealed and wounded areas of our lives spawn word curses and inner vows. Healing the roots of the word curses begins to effectively close the door to Satan and his demonic work in our lives.

Lies of The Enemy

Dr. Ed Smith (1996), Theophostic Healing, believes that it is deeply embedded lies which generally cause a person to feel fearful, abandoned, shamed, tainted, powerless, hopeless, invalidated and confused. Emotions can be triggered in the present, but they are rooted in the past. Smith encourages us to look for the *historical memory event* that feels the same or matches the current emotions. This is to search for the root of these lies or origin of core beliefs. The Holy Spirit will lead us into the truth that displaces the lie we have believed.

Satan was defeated by Jesus Christ at the cross so now all Satan can do is to convince us to believe his lies instead of God's truth. It is the same ploy he used with Adam and Eve. Satan wants us to believe that God's word is not true. In the garden he spoke to Adam and Eve: "Did God really say you must not eat fruit from any tree in the garden?" Not only does Satan want you to think God lies but he wants you to doubt God's loving goodness. Eve explains that if they eat the fruit from the tree in the middle of the garden or even touch it, they will die. Satan says:

> *You will not certainly die, for God knows that when you eat from it your eyes will be opened and you will be like God knowing good and evil*
> **(Genesis 3: 1,4).**

In other words, Satan is leading them in thinking that God doesn't really love them. He doesn't really want them to have an abundant life. God is withholding from them a great gift. Satan challenged Adam and Eve to not just doubt God's Word but to doubt God's love for them and His desire for them to live an abundant life, having a hope and a future in Him. So, it is with us, when difficult storms rise up and we don't get the answer we want or everything seems out of reach, and danger is looming, we are tempted to think God doesn't care, doesn't love us. The disciples with Jesus in the boat with them in the midst of a terrible storm still asked Him the faithless question: *"Don't you care if we drown?"* (Mark 4:38 NIV). The lies of Satan lead to only one outcome - bondage.

At our church, the end of the fiscal year was looming and our financial situation was bleak. How would we pay the salaries? How would we pay the insurance bill and the utilities? The bills were staring us in the face.

The voices of fear came: *We will have to cut staff... We have to rent out the church... We should charge for weddings... We need to charge for healing appointments...* Panic thinking with band-aid solutions were bantered about at the vestry meeting.

Suddenly one wise member began to pray:

> *Lord to whom shall we go; you have the words of eternal life. Show us the way through this financial challenge. You are our Provider. We depend on you and trust you. We repent of looking for our own solutions and not coming to you first. Forgive us. We surrender all the bills to you and the way they will be paid. We surrender all our concerns and worries and accept your love and peace. Thank you for loving us. Amen.*

We actually lifted all the bills up to God, surrendering every one of them. Two weeks later at the end of the year, the treasurer called to inform us that all the money has come in! She said everything is paid and we had a surplus! We went through that same financial scenario several times over our fifteen years together but usually without panic thereafter! We had learned that God is our faithful provider!

In today's world we are told there is no such thing as absolute truth, that all truth is relative. In fact the current thinking is that truth is based on feelings *If it feels good, do it*. It is also popular even among Christians to think that Satan is not real or at least can't harm us. Many Christians believe we don't have to worry about him. C.S. Lewis wrote *The Screw Tape Letters* (originally published in 1942), a religious satire and apologetic novel depicting Satan as taking a subtle approach to tempting Christians. Satan promotes passivity and irresponsibility. His great crafty ploy is for people to think he is just a fantasy figure complete with tail and pitchfork.

According to a Barna poll, 60 percent of American Christians believe he is just a symbol of evil, not a real, living being or person. That statistic amazes me! What that tells me is that the majority of

Christians do not believe the Bible. (http://www.beliefnet.com/Faiths/Galleries/31-Sneaky-Lies-the-Enemy-Wants-You-to-Believe.aspx?p=19#KHHqi2JKFBcqJkdF.99)

Sometimes people have trouble believing that God is really good and can be trusted. How does a lie like that come into our minds and hearts? For some people the open gate originates back to a time in their childhood or even young adulthood when a parent or parents or other authoritative figure in their lives left them, disappointed them or harmed them in some way.

"I've never seen God; never heard God; never been touched by God," exclaimed the tall tattooed twenty-seven year old young man towering over me at the Salvation Army healing prayer meeting. "What am I doing wrong?" he asked. I could see the pain deep in his troubled eyes and etched on his face. Then he said, "Why did Jesus take my father? I need him." His father died of a heart attack when this young man was 21.

"Shall we pray?" Placing my hands on his shoulders I asked the Holy Spirit to take him to this place of deep wounding and pain.

"I see Jesus with my father!" He exclaimed. He was stunned. His Dad was saved! He told his father through Jesus how much he loved him and missed him. He forgave his dad for dying and asked his father to forgive him for the mess he had made of his life.

"Jesus has his arms wrapped around me and my dad," he whispered his eyes tear-filled. Then he opened his eyes and exclaimed that Jesus told me He did not take my father, He received him. The young man burst into tears! To know how much Jesus loved him and his father was over whelming. God hadn't taken his father away. He wasn't a mean God. His dad had cardiac disease and yes, he had died. Jesus didn't cause that. But Jesus was with him when he died and received him into His arms. This was the truth. He asked Jesus to forgive him for blaming Him for his dad's death. And then we prayed for the lies of the enemy to be broken off him and for the Holy Spirit to fill him. By this time he was flat on the floor. A huge grin was plastered across his face.

I leaned over and spoke in his ear: "Let's see you saw God, you heard God and He touched you. Pretty good day don't you think?"

Some of the other lies that Satan wants you to believe are that God doesn't heal or perform miracles anymore. He whispers that you have to be perfect, and God can't or won't forgive your past sins because they are too great. Think of the woman with the alabaster jar.

> *And being in Bethany at the house of Simon the leper, as He sat at the table, a woman came having an alabaster flask of very costly oil of spikenard. Then she broke the flask and poured it on His head.*
> (Mark 14:3-9)

Who was this woman? She was *a woman in the city who was a sinner* Mark tells us. In John's Gospel her sins are paramount for that's all the Pharisaic males who are there talk about. In the Gospels of Matthew and Mark, Judas is more concerned about the waste of costly oil. This sinful woman is rebuked sharply by the leaders in the church. The words ring out as they try to shame her. You can imagine the stinging words, *you could have sold this and given it to the poor!* They imply she is selfish for lavishing this costly perfume on Jesus. What would you do? Have you ever been shamed like this? Would you want to slink away? Can you feel the redness of embarrassment coming over your skin or the lump in your throat as you want to cry? Do you know this shame? As the accusations from an inner voice come to you, the lies begin to take hold of your soul: *I am stupid. I am selfish. I should know better. I can't do anything right.*

In the Gospel of John this woman is rebuked for being a sinner, not just for being a silly, stupid woman. She is a bad woman. All the strikes are against her now. Shamed publicly, all her sins exposed in front of a male audience. The Scarlet letter thrust on her for all to see. Can you feel her head lower in shame? Can you see her eyes averting theirs? Do you know this shame? The lies are embedded deep in her psyche: *I am bad...very bad. There is no hope for me. I will never be free. No one will ever want me.*

She risks everything, her very own life, to come to Jesus. It took courage to enter that room full of men. She carries a small alabaster jar holding precious perfumed oil. Perhaps the jar is also filled with her unmet needs, unhealed hurts, and unresolved issues. Perhaps the jar is filled with collections of inner vows, curses, and lies of the enemy. We all tend to save things.

- We save things that people say to us: usually the hurtful ones…
- We save things that people do to us: usually the hurtful ones
- We save our heart that has been broken tucked away in a safe place, an alabaster jar, though some jars are made of steel.
- We save old arguments, arguing them over and over in our minds. We save old tapes.

We even save the lies of the enemy and believe them:

You deserved it.
  No one needs me.
  No one understands me.
  I'm too fat, too thin…not pretty enough.
  I am just not right.
  I am not enough.
  I am alone.

Maybe her jar is filled with unconfessed sin:
  Secrets: abortion, adulterous affair
  Addictions
  Pornography
  Jealousy

Or was it filled with unforgiveness, resentments, bitterness, broken dreams and broken promises? We know whatever is in that jar is costly.

How is it that this woman can risk all and bring her jar to break at her master's feet? What propels her to take such a risk? Somehow either she has been healed already or knows she is going to be healed by Him. Somehow His love has broken through and now she hears His voice deep in her soul, a voice not of a fairy tale prince but of the King of Kings: *"Come away my beloved and I will heal you, restore you, set you free from your captivity. You were made to be captivating not be captive."*

In the breaking of the jar, she breaks off all the terrible names she has been called, her sordid past and all her desperate behaviors in response. All the idols within are shattered and she finds Him. In the shattering of human dreams, she finds the reality of God. In the shattering of broken promises she finds the promise of God. All these unmet needs and unhealed hurts have compelled her to seek God. All her suffering has become a doorway into God's heart.

As you are reading this Jesus is right here with you. I encourage you to pick up your alabaster jar – it's right in front of you. For some of you it is very heavy. Look inside. It is dark isn't it? What do you see inside? Let Jesus walk you through the contents of your alabaster jar, picture by picture, event by event. Lay it all out, hurts, abandonment, lies, inner vows, word curses, unmet needs, unresolved issues, unhealed hurts, and broken dreams. They all want to come out. The jar is bulging. Watch Jesus. It's time to break the jar you've carried so long. Look at what is coming out of the jar. See the healing pouring forth in you as the pieces fall out. Smell the fragrance pouring forth all over Jesus' feet, all over you. Not what you expected. What happened to all that bitterness and gall inside? In the willingness to break open and pour it all out, Jesus transformed it into beauty. Beauty for ashes is what He does. *It's the great exchange.* You are free, strongholds shattered. All the false expectations, the hurts, disappointments, all the *what ifs* are broken, and the precious suffering made good. The oil of your soul freely poured out on the feet and head of your Savior. What you held so tightly and held you so tightly, now laying in pieces at Jesus feet. It is finished. It is finished. The one who is forgiven much loves much. Watch Jesus. See the pieces. What is He doing? You are His precious alabaster jar and He has transformed you precious child of God, precious dream of God, precious bride of God into His image. Lord seal this healing in Your name: Father, Son and Holy Spirit.

Wrong Sexual and Psychological Soul Ties

Wrong sexual and psychological soul ties that have not been broken and healed are blocks to complete healing of our souls. Sin is wrong behavior. We sin in our thoughts, in our words, and in our deeds. Wrong behaviors occur in every Christian for

> *all have sinned and fall short of the glory of God.*
> **(Romans 3: 23, NIV)**

Wrong behaviors are birthed when we act upon the temptations of the flesh. We will be tempted, for that is Satan's way of getting our attention. Even Jesus was tempted when Satan came to Him in the desert though He never sinned. The decision to give into the temptations and to sin rests with us. (See James 1: 14-16)

Sin separates us from God, not from His love, but from fully (spirit, soul, and body) being in His presence. He is always with us but when we sin we don't know/experience that truth unless we call on Him and repent. God and sin cannot reside in the same space. Sin contradicts the very nature of God.

One wrong behavior is sexual sin. Any sexual act outside of marriage is sin. Fornication, adultery and unbiblical sexual acts are all sexual sins and are wrong in God's eyes. Sexual sin creates harmful sexual and soul ties. You are wrongly united to that person. (See 1 Corinthians 6: 15-20.) It is common for people in our western culture to live together before marriage, like a trial run. According to a report by Focus on the Family, article *The Problem with Living Together, a census reported a 72 % increase in the number of cohabitating couples since 1990*: (Morse, 2001).

Psychological soul ties occur when souls are united. In marriage God makes the two one. This is good. However, there are wrong psychological soul ties. These occur when people are enmeshed or attached in unhealthy ways that cause violation of spiritual, emotional and/or personal boundaries. Some harmful soul ties:

A) Codependent relationships
B) Possessive, controlling relationships
C) Occult relationships
D) Spiritual adulterous relationships (with someone or something other than spouse or God)

You can test yourself about whether a relationship is an unhealthy soul tie or not. If you are married are you sharing intimate conversation with someone other than your spouse? Co-dependent behavior is a pattern of behavior in which you are dependent on approval from another person for your self-worth and esteem. These unhealthy relationships usually depict clinginess and lack of self-sufficiency and autonomy. The other person replaces God. Relationship addiction is another term for codependency. We need to confess, repent, and break any harmful soul ties. Forgive that person and yourself for the harm caused. For many people it is important to have inner healing to get to the root of what unmet need, unhealed hurt, or unresolved issues is driving this behavior,

Prayer for Cutting Soul Ties

In the name of Jesus Christ I renounce and cut with the sword of the Spirit any ungodly soul ties between myself and _____ (you name each one) as a result of (fornication, co-dependency, controlling relationships, spiritual adultery, etc.). It is finished. Amen.

Generational Bondages

The sins of the fathers and mothers travel down the generations to affect the present time, but blessings also travel down the family lines. Jesus' healing power can touch our families with blessing as well as free us from the effects of sin.

> "Patterns of physical, emotional or spiritual sickness can descend upon individuals and families from generation to generation, i.e. diabetes, cancer." (Christian Healing Ministries, 2019).

You shall not bow down to them or worship them; for I, the Lord your God am a jealous God, punishing the children for the sin of the fathers to the third and fourth generation of those who hate me, but showing love to a thousand generations of those who love me and keep my commandments.

(Exodus 20:5-6)

Ezekiel 18 assures us that God doesn't punish children for their parents' sins. God says, *I will judge you, each one according to his ways,* (vs 30). It's not about punishment, it's about what has been deposited generationally. For example, if we took a census of the number of alcoholics in three generations of an alcoholic family paternally, the head count likely would be very high. Why? Because alcoholism was deposited in the family line. This was true in my own family line with my biological father. His mother was alcoholic, he was alcoholic and so was I. A door was left open in past generations for alcoholism to come down the family line to children and grandchildren and great grandchildren until it was confessed, renounced and broken for good in Jesus' Name. We don't have to accept the alcoholism as in my case, but there is a greater temptation or vulnerability to give into this temptation as a way of dealing with the hurts, stress and traumas of this world. Our upbringing and environmental factors will further determine how we respond to the predisposition to addiction in our family line. The test becomes real during difficult times.

Family Line

What negative traits or habits in your life have been in your family line for generations? (Alcoholism, verbal or physical abuse, pornography, racism, bitterness, fear, poverty, illnesses, etc.) These are areas of bondage and strongholds. Anything to which you are genetically predisposed, or any binding influence passed down through the generations can be manifested in your life or your children's lives until confessed and broken by the word of God (sword of the Spirit) and the blood of Jesus Christ.

Strongholds

What is a stronghold? A stronghold is a fortified garrison erected by the enemy to resist truth and God's plan of redemption. Satan can take that one weakness or bad attitude of yours and fence it in and construct a rampart around it. Maybe it's that explosive temper of yours. The stronghold on this temper is old and hangs on. We cannot just grit our teeth and fight harder against this tenacious stronghold. This is how the flesh fights. We have the weapons of God: divine power to demolish strongholds. It's time to let others help you in this struggle.

Confess your sins to each other so that you can live together whole and healed.

(James 5:16 MSG).

A stronghold is what one uses to fortify and defend a personal belief, idea or opinion against outside opposition. (A paraphrase from *Thayer's Greek-English Lexicon*, 2019)

Strongholds protect wrong beliefs, attitudes, and patterns that we have learned to trust. In the beginning they may have been a survival tactic, but if left unchecked they will provide access for the enemy's assaults. We have learned to trust them more than we trust "the truth". Therefore, they must be demolished to allow room for the truth to set us free.

There are many strongholds that build as a way of dealing with our wounds and past traumas of our past. Here are a few: doubt, independence, unforgiveness, false security, control, fear, and denial. These strongholds are walls built around our heart for protection and they not only keep others out but interfere with our relationship with God. Just as no one can get in neither can we get out. These strongholds can seem to protect during traumatic times but now they hinder you from forming intimate caring relationships.

I was praying with an elderly woman who had experienced severe depression and suicidal ideation much of her life. The bondage was great. She brought her pastor with her and most of our time was spent with me sharing and her giving monosyllabic answers if speaking at all. God's Word washed her as I prayed scriptural affirmations over her at the end of our prayer session. She left a little lighter. She was so frightened. Our second session she told me her story of horrible sexual abuse when she was a child. Allowing a little bit of inner healing prayer, slowly walls were coming down. On the last session I had with her, she was still afraid to come out from behind this stronghold. In the room we were using was a large writing pad on a tripod.

In the room we were using was a large writing pad on a tripod. Quickly I stood up and hid behind the pad as if it were a wall. I peeked around at her and she was perplexed. "I'm behind the wall", I said. Suddenly her pastor got up and he too ducked behind the wall with me.

She got up and came behind the wall with us. "Can I join you?" she asked. Are you picturing the three us huddled behind this big notepad? Here she discovered Jesus was with her too. In her minds eye she watched Jesus take the bricks of the stronghold built around her heart out one by one. "I can see through the holes of the bricks He has removed," she said. Freedom was coming!

Generational Strongholds

Generational strongholds can be difficult to recognize, However, they are still in operation even if we don't acknowledge them yet. A young man I knew kept having accidents, one right after another. After a bit of research, he discovered that his father and grandfather were also prone to accidents. Praying through the last three generations on his father's side renouncing and cutting the influence of this debilitating spirit actually stopped the accidents. The word curse, he is *accident prone* was broken too.

We can be free of these generational sins or inherited wounds. The sacrifice of Christ on the cross and God's word are enough to break these strongholds and give us liberty in our lives today as well as our children and grandchildren's lives. We have an inheritance through Jesus Christ. *In Him we have obtained an inheritance.* (Ephesians 1:11). This takes precedence over any natural inheritance. In healing prayer, the Holy Spirit will lead us back to the root of the sin generationally and heal that root no matter how far back it goes. God is outside of time and remember He is with us always. We can repent for our own sins and the sins of our forefathers. Through forgiveness of both we are set free from the consequences of these sins. Hosea 8:7, *They sow the wind and reap the whirlwind.* We no longer have to reap the repercussions of our family sin. Humility is always a key to healing. Every time we humble ourselves, pray, seek God's presence, and turn from our own and our past generations' sinful ways, He does hear us, forgives our sin and heals our land (2 Chronicles 7:14).

Generational bondages are blocks to healing. These bondages are characteristics or patterns that are passed down from one generation to another until there is a breaking and release of the stronghold.

Healing Family History

"One of the most difficult things in life is to gain emotional separateness from that powerful early family environment and not repeat it nor react against it." (Richardson, 1984, p.1). Looking at our family of origin is critical in the process of gaining emotional freedom in Christ. The way we see ourselves, others, and our world view is shaped in the environmental setting of our family. Many of us spoke inner vows in our younger lives stating we would not be or act like our fathers or mothers. Yet, much to our dismay we find ourselves doing the same things our parents did even though we said we wouldn't do these things. It is important to look at our family of origin in the process of healing.

Genogram

One tool that can help us to look back through your generations for unhealed hurts, unmet needs, and unresolved issues is the genogram. A genogram is a diagram of your family. It contains information found on a multi-generational family tree such as names, dates of births and deaths for individuals, marriage dates, siblings, etc. The genogram goes further than a family tree by recording individual characteristics such as personality traits, vocations, marriages and divorces and health. It will also depict the emotional relationships of those same individuals and the emotional patterns of the family system to which they belong. It is best to go back through three generations if you can.

While it is rewarding to find out more about your relatives, the real goal in developing a genogram is an enhanced understanding of yourself. This will allow you to do deeper inner healing work. This is critical for your life today and the life of your family. We tend to either repeat the negative patterns of our family of origin or waste much energy and time in reacting to them. Through Christ's work on the cross, what has gone on before in our family lines that was damaging and hurtful can be healed. These unresolved issues can be resolved in our family history going back three or four generations depending on what the Holy Spirit reveals to you.

Research steps in building your family genogram:

Step One: Starting with you, go back three to four generations if you can. Write down the names and ages of all family members. Give dates of birth and death, marriages, separations, and divorces. Record adoptions, miscarriages, still births, abortions, suicides, even diseases if known.

Step Two: Contact some family members. Ask about relationships. Who was labeled what in the family? Nicknames. Values of family members. Was there a family secret? Who was closer? Who had conflict or showed hostility? Who was cut-off, (left alone, or kicked out, or ostracized)? Was there addiction (Who was it and are they in recovery or not)? Try to develop information about every member in every nuclear family in your extended family. Who was successful? Who wasn't? What impact did the members have on each other? Vocations. Education levels. Who over-functioned? Who under-functioned? How was love expressed? Who carried the legacy in the family? What assumptions were there about gender? You will need to answer these questions too.

When you are doing this research do not challenge or condemn family members and what they share with you. They are giving you their perception and it is probably different from yours. Don't ask *why* questions but *what* questions; i.e. *What did you think about that?*

What you are doing is only a beginning. This work is a life-time process but the understandings will help you know what to bring to prayer so you can become a well-differentiated, emotionally mature person in Christ. This is to grow up into Christ in the lifelong process of sanctification.

Prayer for Cutting Wrong Generational Ties

With the sword of the Spirit cut or sever wrong generational ties back to three generations. If sexual sin is involved through the family line then go back seven generations. Cut and sever these ties between each generation on either or both the paternal and maternal sides. Christ through the power of the Holy Spirit has given us power and authority over unclean spirits, to heal and to have dominion over everything on earth, (Matthew 10:1; Mark 3:15; Genesis 1:26).

Prayer

Father,

I take the sword of the Spirit which is Your living word, and I cut the spirit of wrong generational ties between the third and fourth generation on my mother's side or fathers side or both). - (If you know what spirit of bondage you are breaking like alcoholism, adultery, pornography, divorce, etc. you can insert the following here.) I cut with the sword of the Spirit the spirit of _____ between third and fourth generation, etc.). (Continue praying and cutting through each generation and between the first generation and you. Finally break it between you and your children and your grandchildren or future grandchildren.) At the conclusion of this prayer say: "I seal the ends (imagine a cord that has been broken) with the blood of Jesus Christ never to be joined again. These generational sins now have no power over me or my family. Lord, strengthen my ties to you. Thank you for passing down your blessings through our family line. Thank you, Lord Jesus. Amen

When you are praying this prayer, you may feel resistance between certain generations but continue to pray through for the breaking and it will occur. Also you can pray this same prayer with several wrong generational ties you have discovered in your family research.

A generational stronghold can be: (1) Physical: cancer, diabetes, high blood pressure, etc. (2) Emotional: depression, fear, anxiety, anger, etc. (3) Attitudinal: racism, prejudices, negative self-image, self-hatred and (4) Spiritual: lust, sexual perversion, codependent soul ties, religious spirit, spiritual abuse, etc. These negative strongholds can be broken in our lives! You are not stuck behind them.

> *You shall not bow down to them or serve them, for I the LORD your God am a jealous God... visiting the iniquity of the fathers on the children to the third and the fourth generation of those who hate me, but showing steadfast love to thousands of those who love me and keep my commandments.*
>
> (Exodus 20:5-6 (ESV)

Blessing Prayer

May the Lord God Almighty, bless you with His love that penetrates your heart and pours out through your life. May He bless you with His mercy and kindness drawing others to meet Him through you. May He bless you with His healing oil of gladness that washes over your wounds and makes good out of them all for His glory. May you know now the Lord wraps you in His arms today like He has every day for He is with you always and has never let you go. May the Lord keep you from all harm and cover you under

His healing wings. May you always know God is your stronghold. May God bless you with courage and strength to carry on in His name. May every lie of the enemy you've believed be broken and replaced by His truth living in you which sets you free. May every false stronghold be broken down in your life. May God bless your family that they with you may follow Christ all the days of their lives as long as they live on this earth. May God grant you an abundant life in Him and fulfillment of the plans He has for you, a hope and a future and plans to prosper you. Bless you now in the Name of the Father, Son and Holy Spirit. Amen.

Summation

Blocks to our healing can be healed through the authority and power of Jesus Christ. We are not stuck in our old wounds. Word curses and inner vows must not become self-fulfilling prophecies. We are not paralyzed. In Christ we are new creations and that is our hope.

Chapter 6
FORGIVENESS

The young African woman walked up to me for prayer. She had a swagger - not a cocky swagger - but a holding back swagger that said I really don't want to do this but I'm coming anyway. Her lips closed tightly, holding in whatever she was struggling to say.

"What do you want God to do?" I asked.

She shook her head, stepped back a bit, then came forward again. "I don't know," she said. Her head moved from side to side, her braided pigtails following suit. She had an air about her that exuded confidence and leadership but here she was losing strength, melting down in front of me. The struggle in her soul was evident.

I put my hands on her shoulders and touched her face. I waited. Slowly she began, "I was molested when I was five and horribly and viciously raped when I was eight." Silence followed for a few seconds. She summoned the strength to continue, hands visible but she summoned the strength to continue, "The first was by a family member, the second by a stranger."

My heart hurt with hers. I began to pray. *Come Lord Jesus.* He was already here.

I remained quiet as she saw herself as that wounded young girl. Jesus did not take her to the horror of the rape incident but instead wrapped His arms around this frightened, angry, and deeply hurt eight year old girl still suffering inside this adult woman who was standing in front of me. She felt His presence. Slowly she allowed His peace and love to cover her wounded girl within and adult self simultaneously. Jesus drew her in, wooing her to Himself, encouraging her to receive His love, and begin this painful process of forgiveness so the burden of inner pain would be healed and the accompanying shame lifted off her. Silently I prayed *Lord take this anger that simmers inside her*. After more prayer I gently asked, "Can you forgive the man who did this to you?" Her head shook from side to side…no…no… How could she forgive such a person who afflicted her with such evil?

What is forgiveness? Forgiveness is what brings us back into relationship with God and each other, making it possible for us to walk in unity with Him. And yet it seems to be the most difficult work for us to accomplish. Unforgiveness blocks our true identity. Leanne Payne writes about the need for us all to discover our true center within and there are three major blocks to that discovery in the Triune God: (1) failure to forgive others; (2) failure to receive forgiveness from God; and (3) failure of self-acceptance (*Healing Presence*, Payne, 1995, 82). It's all about forgiveness.

Forgiveness is a Choice

Forgiveness is a choice, a difficult one at times, but still a choice. Forgiveness is one of our most basic needs but the *central feature of forgiveness is its radical gift character. Forgiveness can only occur when freely given away* (Oden, 2009, p 594). Oden citing Origen and Calvin, points out the cost of this forgiveness for the one forgiving cancels the debt, forfeiting that which is due and taking responsibility for any liability or deficit. God's forgiveness then involves God taking our sins upon Himself and bearing them on the cross. Jesus proclaims a radical message of the forgiveness of God and the forgiveness we must have for each other. (May, 1988, p114).

How does this radical act of Christ's forgiveness and self-sacrifice speak to healing? *The greatest block to receiving healing at the deepest level is unforgiveness* (Kraft, 1993, p 152). Forgiveness means, *Thou shall not nail another to his past* (Augsburger, 1996, p 3). Forgiveness is key to healing. *What I have come to see... is how intimately the forgiveness of sins is connected with bodily and emotional healing* (MacNutt, 1974, p 135). While praying with a man who had been diagnosed with bladder cancer, the Spirit rose up in me and suddenly I asked, "Who haven't you forgiven?"

"Myself" he quietly said. He explained the reason and as he did Jesus poured His love into him He felt His blessed assurance of forgiveness and grace. Tears of pain mingled with soul surrender gave way to peace and lifting of his whole demeanor. Hope arose and love prevailed. We prayed for him for physical healing of his bladder. A few weeks later he texted me, *I've been to my cancer doctor to set up my surgery. He decided to take another look inside the bladder before surgery. He looked and looked again. There's no cancer. It's gone.* Forgiveness and healing intertwined. Forgiveness involves the quality of being with another in spite of injury done or alienation experienced. Leanne Payne (1991) would reference this *being with another* as acknowledging the Presence of God who is truly present (p25).

Secular, medically approved studies done worldwide, link cancer to unexpressed anger and the link to forgiveness as the key to getting well. Kings College Hospital in London gave a detailed psychological review administering questionnaires to 160 breast cancer patients. They discovered a significant association between the diagnosis of breast cancer and a dysfunctional behavior pattern of extreme suppression of emotions throughout their lives. Anger was the most prevalent emotion suppressed (Greer & Morris, 1975). Other studies have been done by the College of Nursing, University of Tennessee, Department of Psychology, University of Miami, Department of Epidemiology, and the School of Public Health, University of Michigan all showing similar results. They all agreed there was a strong correlation between suppression of emotions and low cancer survival rates. Colin C.Tipping, Founder/Director of The Georgia CancerHelp Program and Together-We-Heal, Inc. suggests in an article *Radical Forgiveness – A Complementary Treatment for Cancer* that supports and proposes that emotional spiritual healing for people with cancer is a strategy for survival. Forgiveness is a major component of the treatment for cancer. They make a distinction between using only the current fear-based approach to cancer which usually addresses symptoms and physical root causes and does not include emotional healing and radical forgiveness which allows the patient to embrace the cancer and address the emotional root causes.

Spiritually radical forgiveness is accomplished through the work of the cross and the shed blood of Jesus Christ for our sins. His radical forgiveness, received and embraced into our being, creates the inner atmosphere for us to love as radical forgivers in this world. Who knew what an antidote to cancer is so within our reach!

Ruth Carter Stapleton (1977) in her book, *The Experience of Inner Healing*, suggests an interesting and disturbing consequence of unforgiveness: We become what we can't forgive. By rejecting another person and refusing to forgive we are refusing to look at the root problem within ourselves. The consequence is deeper repression of our personal weakness and an increased tendency to express that weakness without realizing it. Whatever we cannot forgive we are doomed one day to live. The person who refuses to forgive the gossip eventually becomes a gossip. One who cannot forgive a betrayal becomes a betrayer. The reason for this is that the inability to forgive a frailty in another person indicates that we have the same negative condition existing in us (p 62-63).

Furthermore, the inability to forgive can lead to the wounded person seeking revenge on the perpetrator or whoever reminds them of the perpetrator. This allows evil to fully triumph: *To triumph fully, evil needs two victories, not one. The first victory happens when an evil deed is perpetrated; the second victory when evil is returned* (Volf, 2006, p 9). Forgiveness is the antidote to the disease of evil.

I looked at the young African woman still standing in front of me and noticed the tears coming down her cheeks. She wasn't sobbing loudly but quietly weeping. I asked her again, "Are you willing to forgive this man so you will no longer be in bondage to him? You are not forgiving his behavior you are releasing him from your judgement and giving him to Jesus to deal with."

She looked at me, "Do I have to say it out loud?"

When you speak forgiveness for another out loud, the unforgiveness loses its power. And you may need to do this quite a few times in your life but each time you will be freer than the time before.

Slowly, haltingly she started with little volume at first but it built toward the end of her statement, "I forgive you. What you did was wrong. You hurt me, but I forgive you and release you from my judgement. You are set free to Jesus and so am I."

We prayed for Jesus to cleanse her inside out and she began to feel the shame washing off her. The rage that lived in her, began to come out as her body shook. We cast out that spirit of rage in the name of Jesus Christ as His love simultaneously began to fill her, bending her soul now to Jesus and not to the horrific trauma in her past. The Holy Spirit surged through her and she dropped to the floor, God's love continuing to fill her soul, healing the wounds and deep hurt by His own wounds for *by His wounds we are healed*, (Isaiah 53:5). Her deep pain subsided.

I asked, "What do you feel when you think of this man?"

She responded I feel nothing...just peace. Peace registered on her face. Yes, forgiveness is a choice and she made it. She is no longer a victim but a victor. She is now a Alleluia!

Why Do We Need to Forgive?

The Lord's Prayer states as taught by Jesus, *forgive us our trespasses as we forgive those who trespass against us*. Jesus taught it and demonstrated it by His final act of sacrificial love on the cross. With His arms outstretched on the cross held by nails driven into His hands in excruciating pain, He spoke, *Father, forgive them for they know not what they do* (Luke 23: 34a). He didn't just model forgiveness, He became forgiveness. He personified forgiveness. He forgave while being wounded and killed. His forgiveness is greater than the offense inflicted upon Him.

Remember the two crucified thieves who were on both sides of Jesus? One hurled abuse at him but the other thief rebuked that thief and defended Jesus saying

> *this man has done nothing wrong. Jesus remember me when you come into your kingdom,*
>
> **(Luke 23:41-42 NAS).**

Jesus responded *Truly I say to you, today you shall be with me in paradise,* (Verse 43). Forgiveness is a decision of the heart. As Jesus forgives this thief, he is released from his sins into the arms of Jesus.

Forgiveness doesn't mean the offender's behavior is condoned, acceptable or appropriate but your forgiveness of the one who hurt you releases you from the bondage of unforgiveness and releases the other from your judgment which belongs to God. The one who hurt you may still face legal consequences, if appropriate. But that is no longer your focus.

Forgiveness is Our Calling

Forgiveness is our calling. We are called to live as forgiven and forgiving children and that is radically inclusive. (John 13:34-35; Luke 6:35). The demands for forgiveness are so daunting that they seem humanly impossible like the horrible situation of the African young woman. Forgiveness is simply beyond the capacity of ungraced human will. Only reckless confidence in a source greater than ourselves can empower us to forgive the wounds inflicted by others. In hard, difficult times like this, there is only one place to go – the cross of Calvary.

There on the cross Abba's only begotten Son died completely alone in bloody disgrace. Again and again God brings me to the crucifixion of my Lord and Savior, Jesus Christ. Again God reminds me that in Christ's final moments of life, He breathes out forgiveness on His tormentors. Listen again. *Father forgive them for they know not what they are doing.* It is here we experience the healing power of the dying Lord. Remember He did this while he was suffering. It was not spoken after the fact but during His horrible suffering at the tormentors' hands. Forgiveness is costly. It cost Jesus His life.

The inner healing of the heart takes time. It is a gradual growing into oneness with the Crucified One. It will happen but it takes time because memories are so vivid and hurts so deep. However we know these memories can be healed through Jesus Christ. God gives us new vision replacing the old pictures of pain. God does replace the pictures that are so painful, those etched in visons of painful events. How does this happen? Jesus is seen in the unhealed memory by the one being prayed for. This changes the whole perspective of the event. Once His light invades these dark places, they can no longer inflict pain or turmoil. The event happened and the picture is there, but you now see it from a kingdom perspective. The evil has lost its power and its influence on your life.

Through forgiveness your heart will be healed from bitterness, anger, resentment, and hatred. This healing is only through Christ who is the power and wisdom of God, a living force in His present risenness. Through Christ our lives are transformed which enables us to extend the hand of reconciliation toward our enemies. Healed memories are now experienced and seen through Jesus Christ.

Some events are so traumatic and horrific in people's lives it seems impossible for a hand of reconciliation to be extended toward a perpetrator. But with God all things are possible even with the group of Rwandans that were gathered here with us for a week-long conference on healing. Does God heal? Yes and after each teaching session and ministry, the witness of God healing deep wounds of rejection and abandonment were seen through their tears, followed by joyful dancing.

Back in 1994, in the country of Rwanda, during a 100-day period from April 7th through mid July, approximately one million Tutsis were slaughtered by the Hutu majority. This represented about twenty percent of the nation's population. The people attending our healing conference in 2009 in Rwanda were Hutus and Tutsis, both victims and released prisoners. The third day of the conference I was scheduled to teach on forgiveness to be followed by ministry time. Suddenly the afternoon before I was to teach, I came down with a severe intestinal illness. *The devil prowls around like a roaring lion seeking someone to devour.* (1 Peter 5:8). No doubt he had come after me. We were staying at a campground and our hosts graciously gave us the best they had to offer but it was not a comfortable place to be sick. As I lay on the almost flat foam mattress, I prayed. My team prayed. People back home prayed. *Should we take her to the hospital?* I overheard outside my door. Too weak to answer aloud, yet inside my heart and mind rose up the scripture, *no weapon formed against me shall prosper,* (Isaiah 54:17).

The next morning after a rough night, two young Rwandan women came to my door and said ever so gently, "Pastor it is almost time for you to teach."

After eating a bit of pineapple and banana, I dressed and was ready. As I walked out the door, I began to sing, "I walk by faith, each step I take, I put my trust in you." Trust me, I meant every word of that song physically as well as spiritually! *Submit to God, resist the devil, and he will flee from you,* (James 4:7). I walked into the packed room, all was silent.

The Anglican priest looked at me. "You don't look so good," he said.

I just smiled. My southern grandmother would have said I looked like death warmed over. The local pastor prayed over me before I began teaching on forgiveness. My translator and I exchanged glances of confidence and assurance. *Faith is confidence in what we hope for and assurance about what we do not see,* (Hebrews 11:1). The living word of God was a reality right there in that place. Together we began to teach and the demonstrative work of the Lord began to rise up in me. Stronger and stronger the message came. Color came back into my cheeks and soon I was on fire for the Lord. The people listened with rapt attention, leaning forward in their seats. The team sat stunned. The healing of my body which they all witnessed caught them up into Him to receive His message of forgiveness and healing in their own souls. We preach Christ crucified. Signs and wonders follow; God in action.

Later that day back in our large group gathering after small group ministry time, people came forward to share their witnesses of what God had done that day. One small woman came forward holding hands with another woman who had been a perpetrator telling the ravaging crowd running through the village with machetes where families were hiding. They were all killed except this one woman who had escaped and the perpetrator. . She looked at the woman next to her who stood with her head hanging down, and taking her hand softly said, "You are my sister. What I am wearing today is yours to keep. I forgive you." You could hear a pin drop in that room.

This healing is only through Christ who transforming our lives, enables the hand of reconciliation to be extended to our enemies. The next day

I taught on reconciliation. Oh what dancing broke out as barriers of old prejudices, past violence and deep wounding were torn down. The enemy had been defeated again with this people, in this place, in this time. Once again what Christ accomplished on the cross was manifested that day.

Unforgiveness

What is unforgiveness? Unforgiveness is essentially a lack of love. Unforgiveness is bondage. *Unforgiveness is like dirt or filth on our inner man.* (Joyce Myers, Life in the Word, June 11, 2002 televised teaching). It has been said that unforgiveness is like drinking poison and then waiting for the other person to die. Unforgiveness is destructive to the person who holds it in his/her heart, breeding resentments, bitterness, and the desire for revenge. It brings darkness and oppression to the soul instead of light and peace.

Set us free, O God, from the bondage of sin and give us the liberty of that abundant life which you have made known to us in your Son our Savior Jesus Christ, who lives and reigns with you, in the unity of the Holy Spirit, One God, now and forever. Amen. (Book of Common Prayer, p. 216)

One of the hardest things for us humans to do is to forgive. Why is this so? Somehow we think that by not forgiving a person we are punishing them. Many people don't even know someone has not forgiven them. The truth is that we are the ones wounded and punished by the unforgiveness. Acid eats the container it is put in faster than the container it is sprinkled on. You and I are not designed by God to be containers of unforgiveness. If we hold onto unforgiveness, it will eat away at the very core of our soul.

Do we think by forgiving them, we are condoning their behavior? Actually by forgiving them we give up judging them which is God's work and we actually hand them over to God who already has hold of them. I hear people say *I have a right to be angry! A right not to forgive!* Not really, according to what Jesus teaches. The formula is there in the Lords Prayer. *Forgive us our debts as we forgive our debtors* (Matthew 6:9-13 KJV) We receive forgiveness as we forgive others. We have a right to refuse Gods forgiveness but is that beneficial or productive in our lives as followers of Christ? None of this seems fair as if someone is getting away with something. Trusting God with the process of forgiveness is the only way no matter how egregious the offense. This is the way through, walking a life of forgiveness. Forgiveness is a lifestyle.

I was assigned to hospice for my internship toward the end of my master's program in Psychology and Counseling through Nova University, FL. All my clients were house-bound. One man in particular was extremely angry and negative toward life and everyone around him. His wife suffered from this man's constant barrage of belittling remarks aimed at her. One of the difficult parts of hospice counseling is that you always have to have closure with each client at the end of every session for you may not see them again. One afternoon as he was spewing forth his anger, I asked him, "Who are you so angry at?" It stunned him. To give you a fuller picture of this scene, he was sitting on the porta-potty at the time with me in the room. He shot a quick look at me and said, "My father, that's who I am angry at."

This client was in his late 70's and he began to tell a story of what had happened to him when he was 15 years old. The whole family was going on a picnic which was an incredible treat since they had little money. Before leaving, the father went to the basement to retrieve something and discovered one of his tools laying on the work bench broken. He came storming back upstairs and demanded to know who had broken it. My client knew his younger brother had done it but he didn't want his father to hurt him so he spoke up and said to his father that he did it.

Immediately his father banished him to the basement, locking the door and shouted through the door, "You are not going on the picnic. You will stay where you are until we get back." At this point in the story all the pent up anger and hurt came pouring forth. I prayed silently asking God to reveal himself to this broken man. I saw his fifteen year old self so bound up with anger and bitterness. I prayed and prayed. Suddenly he knew he could forgive. Only God can do this with another. Through the tears he forgave his father and his brother too. At the end of our session he forgave himself for holding this for so long and dishonoring his own father. He was set free. He died two weeks later.

I went back to visit with his wife after the funeral and she told me with tears streaming down her face that the last two weeks had been the best years of their married life. Explaining how God somehow extended their time together, she shared the confessions they expressed to each other, the deep forgiveness given as their hearts were healed and they became one.

Other obstacles to forgiveness within us are pride, self-blame, emotional investment, false identity, judgment, self-righteousness, anger at God, repression, shame, guilt, and perceived loss to name a few.

> *But God proves his love for us in that while we still were sinners Christ died for us*
>
> **(Romans 5:8)**

The cost of remaining in unforgiveness is high. Imagine yourself standing next to the person you are unwilling to forgive. A rope is tied around your waist because you are bound up by the unforgiveness in you. However, you are not only bound up yourself, but you are bound to the one you haven't forgiven. You are bound by unforgiveness. Everywhere you go you drag that person with you. You are not free until you forgive. What is the cost of unforgiveness?

The cost of unforgiveness is many fold: (1) you will remain emotionally tied to the hurtful event in your past and to the one who hurt you and this event will play over and over in your mind like a bad tape; (2) you will be hurt over and over again as this plays through your mind because you are bound to this hurtful event and the one who hurt you; (3) your relationship with God and others will be negatively impacted; and (4) your spiritual and emotional growth is stunted for you cannot move on successfully.

The antidote to unforgiveness is forgiveness. This sounds so obvious yet it is so difficult when the wounding is deep. It was not easy for me to forgive the father of my son who had walked out on our marriage. As I worked through the twelve steps of Alcoholics Anonymous with my sponsor, she asked me, "Are you willing to forgive your ex-husband?" Very quickly I responded, "No!"

She didn't give up. Again, she asked me but with a bit of a twist, "Are you willing to be willing to forgive?"

My answer had not changed. It was still no. Yet she wasn't finished with me for she asked if I was willing to be willing to be willing to forgive him.

Astonished, I asked her "What about no are you not getting?" I was a bit of a smart aleck even in sobriety.

She had the nerve to go back to seven 'willings'. Are you willing, to be willing, to be willing, to be willing, to be willing, to be willing, to be willing?

Exhausted I surrendered, "Fine!Yes!"

It was all God needed to open that crack in my heart to begin the process of deep forgiveness and healing within me.

Forgiveness of Self

What about forgiveness of ourselves? The man in the back of the room at the Salvation Army wasn't very noticeable by dress or looks but I happened to see him while I was praying with someone. He was waiting patiently for others to be ministered to before he came up to me. He stood in front of me, hands clasped tightly, head slightly down and said in a matter of fact, staccato fashion with little emotion, "I murdered my father... It was premeditated. He was an evil man. He beat my mother and he beat me. I knew he was going to kill her someday... I was seventeen years old. Our family priest spoke up for me and the courts acquitted me... But I murdered my own father." We both stood silent for a bit.

Forgiving oneself is difficult. I'm not talking about hurried mental confessions. I'm talking about deep heart-felt painful admissions of sins in front of God and one other person. It seems impossible to do. Yet unforgiveness of self is a failure to receive forgiveness from God and this failure to receive forgiveness from God has to do with our own negative inner vision of ourselves and the failure to acquire self-acceptance (Payne, 1991, 82). By receiving forgiveness from God, we no longer identify ourselves by the sin from which we have been delivered and healed. The sin no longer has the power to name us. How do we know we have forgiven ourselves and others?

Reconciliation: Expression of Forgiveness

Forgiveness is ultimately expressed in reconciliation with God, with others when possible, and oneself. ... *authentic forgiveness is that cluster of motivations which seeks to regain the brother or sister in reconciliation* (Augsburger, 115). The Christian ministry of reconciliation takes place among the very sinners whom Christ came to call to righteousness. *Is there reasonable hope for reconciliation not only with my wounded past but also with those who have wronged me...?* (Volf, 2006, 43). This is the question of healing that lingers in our hearts and minds challenging the progress of healing within each of us.

Reconciliation is God's action *reconciling the world to Himself in Christ* (2 Cor. 5.19). *While we were still sinners, Christ died for us,* breaking the sin/death syndrome thru Christ's atoning death and resurrection (Rom 5.8). What does this mean for us? Augustine stated the *saving event is not about God receiving our gifts, but God giving His own Gift, His Son, in order to offer us the benefit of salvation* (Oden, Classic Christianity 406).

Reconciliation is the process of bridging the uncrossable gap of estrangement between us and God due to sin by the self-sacrificing work of Christ. God once again becomes *'friendly'* with us after estrangement (John 15.13-15). He has settled our differences with Him, putting us into the process of becoming compatible with Him and the Body of Christ through the sanctifying power of the Holy Spirit. The means of atonement and reconciliation of God with us is Christ; the end is not counting sins (Oden 407). John Chrysostom in a Homily on Romans 5.1-11, states, *Reconciliation is the restoration of the justified to communion with God* (407).

If we do not receive the reconciling work of Christ as personal redemption, how do we reconcile individually to God and to each other? There must be a human response. From God's side atonement is a finished act and from our side we must receive this reconciling event already accomplished by God, and allow it to be accomplished in us. This requires a behavioral reversal (Oden, 2009, p 407). Augsburger (1996) suggests that this response is conciliation which is the work while reconciliation is the hoped-for outcome (Augsburger, 1996, p116). This work of the Holy Spirit within us is the process of sanctification.

What was this man standing in front of me who had murdered his father as a teenager looking for from God? "Can God forgive me? I know murder is sin," he painfully asked. While it was no longer possible for physical reconciliation with his father it was possible for spiritual reconciliation with God, and through God with his earthly father and himself. We prayed.

Suddenly, as he began to sink down to the floor on his knees, he shared haltingly, "Jesus is standing here with me. His arm is around my shoulders." He didn't expect that. He saw himself as that scared seventeen year old boy who didn't know Jesus back then. But suddenly he was with Jesus. Instantly the forgiveness of God washed over him and tears began to run down his face. With his face to the floor, he confessed through tears, "I didn't want to murder him but I had to. I didn't know to ask You how to work this out Jesus. I didn't know You Jesus." But Jesus knew him. Deeper and deeper God's love washed through him, releasing him from long pent up grief and the deep need to confess and repent.

God's love washed the wounds from his abused childhood. Like a photo album being opened up he saw Jesus actually washing his wounds where his father had beat him, dressing them, and healing them. This is not hard for God to do for he lives outside of time and the past is not past if it is still causing you havoc in your present life. In a moment of full surrender, he asked through God for his father to forgive him for murdering him. Though his father had brutally abused him and his mother, he still wanted forgiveness. Suddenly he looked up at me and said, "The pain of all those years of abuse is gone!" There with Jesus, he forgave himself and the weight of grief and guilt lifted off his shoulders. He received the reconciling work of Jesus Christ into himself. Joy broke out on his face! The pure, wonderful joy of God broke through and the sorrow that had lasted so long was now gone. Alleluia!

"Forgiveness is the remission of sins. For it is by this that what has been lost, and was found, is saved from being lost again." St Augustine of Hippo (St Augustine R. C. Church, 2019)

Summation

Who do you need to forgive? Picture a cross in front of you. It might be a picture of a special cross you love or one you've seen outdoors or one that's in your church. Let that picture come into your mind. Place yourself in front of that cross. Are you standing, kneeling or laying down? Remember Jesus is with you always, so He is present with you right now at the cross. Ask Him to manifest Himself to you if you don't sense or see Him. Take your time. When you are ready, let the one you need to forgive come into this picture. Remember you are with Jesus so you are completely safe. Watch Jesus with this person. What is Jesus doing? Come a little closer. Ask whatever you want to ask keeping your eyes on Jesus. Are you ready to forgive? Just a willingness is a beginning. Look at the one who hurt you and when ready say, "I forgive you. What you did was wrong" (and list some things) "but I forgive you and I release you from my judgment. You are set free to Jesus and I am set free too." Sit with this. Let the forgiveness wash over you. All the pain and bitterness flows out of you as forgiveness flows in. You may need to forgive yourself. There may be others you need to forgive. You can go through this same process again with each one. Remember forgiveness is accomplished at the cross.

Thank you, Jesus, for your forgiveness. We seal this healing in the name of the Father, Son, and Holy Spirit. Amen

Chapter 7
SPIRITUAL AUTHORITY AND WARFARE

Spiritual Authority

Then Jesus came and spoke to them, saying, 'All authority has been given to Me in heaven and on earth.'

(Matthew 28:18)

What is authority? The internet dictionary states that authority is the power or right to give orders, make decisions, and enforce obedience. It is delegated from one person or organization to another. Strong's Concordance says authority is privilege and delegated influence. Authority itself is not power but it is the right given to use and wield that power. Jesus states in the Matthew scripture that all authority has been given to Him to use in both heaven and earth. His Father gave Him that privilege and right to exercise power. Interestingly authority in the kingdom goes hand in hand with submission which seems like an oxymoron. Jesus submitted Himself even unto death. *And being found in human form, he humbled himself by becoming obedient to the point of death, even death on a cross,* (Philippians 2:8 ESV). The root word in authority is author and since

God is the Author of all creation, therefore He gives the authority. Then he called his twelve disciples together and gave them power and authority over all devils and to cure diseases, (Luke 9:1). It is authority done in Jesus' name. (Luke 10:17; Mark 16:17; Acts 3:6)

How do you receive power and authority? First, Jesus called His disciples together. He gathered them to Himself. They belong to Him. In order to receive God's power and authority you must know you belong to Him. As I have prayed with different people over the years this theme of not belonging and not fitting in is expressed frequently. The group of volunteers that helped me research my doctoral thesis on relapse in inner healing shared these deep wounds:

> *I (sic) never felt like I belonged; always on the outside looking in.*
>
> *I (sic)… was put in boarding school for 2 years after grandfather died; then lived with an elderly woman the last 2 years of schooling… felt not wanted, abandoned.*
>
> *A few years ago, I had the opportunity to reconnect with my mother's favorite cousin. At that time, she voiced for me my family situation. She said, 'Honey, it's like you are an orphan!', even though my parents were both still alive at the time. It really hit me, because that rang true to my spirit.*

I don't fit in.

Nobody wants me.

There is no one there for me.

These statements reflect an orphan spirit operating in their lives which prevents us from receiving love and the knowledge we belong to God, thus making it difficult to trust Him. This prevents us from receiving the authority and power he gives us.

Orphan Spirit

What is a spiritual orphan? A spiritual orphan is one who feels alone, does not belong and does not feel loved. This person doesn't feel or know he or she is safe in the Father's heart and thus is filled with fear, insecurity and anxiety.

Why can't these people receive the Fathers love? They have been hurt, wounded, abused, rejected and abandoned by their earthly fathers and /or mothers, the ones who have authority over them. This deep wounding within prevents them from trusting God, since they don't trust the earthly authority figures over them. We cannot receive love if we don't trust the one(s) giving it. Trust involves receiving and receiving involves vulnerability. These unhealed hurts and unmet needs must be healed in order for trust to be established which is the core issue for spiritual orphans.

Do you rise up every morning feeling like a son or daughter secure and confident in your Father's love and living to give that love to others? Or do you get up every day feeling like a slave, struggling constantly with fears of failure or rejection, unable to trust? The journey of healing is about us moving from slavery to freedom,

You know you are loved when you get up in the morning feeling so loved and accepted in your Father's heart that your whole purpose for existence becomes looking for ways to give that love away to the next person you meet. (Frost, 2006)

We live our life either as if we have a home or we don't. We can live feeling safe or we can live in fear and uncertainty. Three fears common to all of us are: fear of trusting, fear of rejection, and fear of exposing our heart to love. Which fear applies to you? When did this fear begin? If one's heart is not healed, it can become a stronghold of oppression which only the Father's love can dismantle.

Remember the testimony I shared about finding my adoption papers in the glove compartment of our car when I was in seventh grade? I saw in black and white that I was adopted by my father, even my last name had been changed. All of a sudden, I didn't know who I was any more. I didn't belong to my father! Who am I? Who is my real father? The anger and the fear rose up in me for I had been living a lie. My father was not my biological father. My heart began to close up, afraid to trust. Not knowing how to handle this upheaval, I threw myself into every musical and athletic activity and leadership positions I could. I excelled. I had to. My identity depended on it. Some of you reading this know what I mean. God has healed me of this orphan spirit starting back at the womb and through several other healing prayer times later. I eventually learned to trust God and finally began to trust authority figures in my life, but it took time. Today I am a woman both under authority and in authority in which I find great freedom.

Adam and Eve: Origin of Orphan Spirit

All of us are born with an orphan spirit that exhibits itself by our rejection of parental authority and our desire to do things our way. I remember my granddaughter at age two expressing the infamous No from time to time. The only ones who were not born with an orphan spirit were Adam and Eve for they were born with a spirit of sonship. When they chose to rebel against God by believing the lie of Satan, they exchanged the spirit of sonship for the orphan spirit. The serpent asked, *Did God really say, 'you must not eat from any tree in the garden?'* (Genesis 3:1 NIV). Eve affirmed that. But the serpent immediately had her doubt God's word, in fact God's love. He put across the false idea that if God really loved you He would give you everything. They both bit the bait, choosing to walk away from God. Their sin became exposed to them through each other.

Adam and Eve hide from God because they are ashamed. Shame has been with us from this time forth. Shame is when you became more conscious of your own flesh than of the Father's love for you. Flesh is that perspective of life developed by the orphan spirit in us. Jack Frost (2006) asserts that Adam and Eve have introduced into the human race, a fatherless mentality. If you think you have no father, you will set yourself apart from our heavenly Father and strive in a way to find one here on earth. Unhealed orphans strive for love, affection and fatherly affirmation and blessing. I did. Orphans many times make inner vows like: *I have to take care of myself,* and *I have to be the provider.* These inner vows further separate them from God and His love as they take on God's role. If one cannot trust God, one cannot receive the love He has for you nor His power and authority. Orphans are driven people by fear, pride, and ambition. Sons and daughters are drawn by God to follow and are free to respond to God, their Father. *"I will not leave you orphans, I will come to you"* (John 14:18). This is the truth!

What are the hallmarks of an orphan spirit?
- Inability to have lasting relationships
- Hatred of authority, general distrust for leaders
- General lack of direction for your life
- Inability to make key, strategic decisions
- Drawing near, then backing away from intimacy
- A sense that they're just going to reject you anyway
- A gnawing sense of failure, never quite good enough
- An inexplicable drive to succeed, win, prove yourself (Frost, 2016)

How to receive healing for an orphan spirit:
1. Recognize this orphan spirit and be willing to expose it. If you do not see that you have it, you may never be set free. So, the first step is revelation.

2. Ask Jesus to be with you in these past hurts of feeling abandoned and rejected and reach out to Him for full healing.
3. Forgive those who abandoned you.
4. Ask God to forgive you for any anger, bitterness, blame you are holding against yourself or others. Be sure to forgive yourself.
5. Release your expectations to Jesus that people will abandon you. Ask the Holy Spirit to guide your friendships and relationships.
6. Trust God. Begin to build friendships.

We are all adopted. *But you have received the spirit of adoption* (Rom 8:15 c.f. Gal. 4:5). We have all suffered with doubt about belonging to the family of God. And the Church has many mentors, but few fathers. God knew this would happen so He gave us the spirit of adoption. The very spirit of God, who teaches us how to pray, gives us the confidence to cry *Abba, Father.*

In ancient Israel, sometimes adoption contracts were written which involved the responsibility of both the adopter and adoptee. This was a solemn declaration with these words by the adoptee: *You are my father and you are my mother.* The adopter declared these words, *You are my son.*

> *And a voice came from heaven: 'You are my Son, whom I love, with you I am well pleased (Mark 1:11)*
>
> *And I will be a Father to you and you will be my sons and daughters, says the Lord Almighty (2 Corinthians 6:18)*

Faith and Authority

True authority is given not taken. The Pharisees confronted Jesus as He was teaching with the question: *By what authority are you doing these things? And who gave you this authority?'* (Matthew 21:23). Jesus didn't tell them, but we know that His authority was given to Him by his Father.

Part of seminary training for most denominations is a course called Clinical Pastoral Education (CPE). The requirement is that the seminarian works as a chaplain in a hospital or similar setting for twelve weeks. This entailed my summer between my first year and second year of seminary. I arrived at Erlanger Hospital ready and eager to begin my internship. However, on the way home from that first orientation day I began to feel ill and a few hours later ended up in the ER of the local hospital. Diverticulitis was the diagnosis. Surgery seemed imminent. My seminarian friends prayed. People back home in Florida prayed. And on the third day I made a turn for complete recovery through prayers and antibiotics. Much to the surprise of the doctors I was released from the hospital two days later. The following Monday I hit the floor running at the hospital.

"Quickly come, Sharon," the chair of our CPE group said to me. I had been assigned several areas of the hospital as my domain to cover and one was the ICU waiting room. A young man, sixteen years old, had been flown in by helicopter from Alabama with head trauma from a near fatal car accident. My supervisor led me to the doctor in charge who pulled me aside and said, "Prepare his family for his death." The doctors didn't expect him to last 24 hours. What? *Please Lord Jesus...please.* I stood outside the ICU with this young man's mother, ready to go in and pray with him. He was in a coma. I prayed so hard, *Lord what do I say?* A ticker tape message floated across my heart, *In the name of Jesus Christ you are healed!* I inwardly gasped. That might be me. After all, my son was fifteen years old at the time and just had his learners driving permit. I prayed again and the message repeated, *In the name of Jesus Christ you are healed!*

They opened the door to let me in and I stood beside this lanky southern teen age boy full of tubes, laying there in a coma. What my eyes saw was not encouraging. His mother across the bed from me reached out and touched my hand. I began to pray. I had no intention of saying what God had given me out in the hallway, but suddenly out of my mouth came *in the Name of Jesus Christ you are healed!* His arm suddenly jerked upward. Now I know medically they tell you that's the nerves involuntarily responding, but I knew it was the Lord and so did his mother. Once outside of ICU I said to her, "I don't know what I'm doing but I will keep on doing it as long as God gives me that!" As she wept, she took Jesus in her heart as her Lord and Savior right there in that hallway with me. What a first day of CPE.

The next day our seminarian group consisting of two Church of God seminarians, one Lutheran, one 7th Day Adventist and two Episcopalians (I'm one) and our director who was Disciples of Christ, met for us to share our verbatims, detailed reflections of events we've faced in our chaplaincy encounters with patients. It was my turn. Girding up my courage I shared about what happened with this young man in ICU when I was praying. Suddenly one of the seminarians jumped up out of his seat and loudly responded, "By whose authority do you say that?" Stunned I responded, "Not mine!"

That first twenty-four hour period passed by and so did many other twenty-four hour periods pass by. Every day I went to see him and prayed the words God gave me back in the beginning of this boy's healing journey. His mother stayed at the Ronald McDonald house the whole time and brought many people to Christ in the ICU waiting room. She shared with me on one of our many talks that her son was the religious one in the family. He used to play Amazing Grace on his guitar. Now she was living it.

Many opportunities were given to stretch our faith. *His lungs are filling up,* the mother told me. Again we called every Christian radio station and churches from all over. Suddenly the lungs returned to normal. Again the frantic call came, *his liver is shutting down!* Intercession increased! The doctor came in and said, "I don't want to know what you are doing but the liver is regenerating itself!" Praise God after praise God came from our lips. One day while I was in his room praying, I saw his eyes follow me. *Oh my, you're in there!* I was overjoyed! Soon they moved him out to a regular room but didn't hold much hope for neurological improvement but once again prayer changed that too.

After my three-month stint at Erlanger ended, I headed back to seminary, and he headed to the rehabilitation center. Before I left the hospital to return to seminary, the director of our CPE unit pulled me aside and told me that I was the first chaplain the doctors and nurses had allowed in the ICU for ten years. Stunned I asked why. Apparently, some commotion had erupted during a chaplain's prayer time visit, disturbing the staff and patients, and they stopped all future chaplains from visiting. Somehow God protected, guided, and held me incognito! What a great bonus to this whole faith walk of healing with this young man and his family.

One month after returning to seminary my phone rang. On the other end came the sweet southern drawl of that young man's mother. "Hey Sharon, someone wants to talk with you." My heart stopped and swallowing hard I heard, "Hey Sharon, my mama told me all about you and what you did. I don't remember anything but thank you. Wait a minute I have something for you." And suddenly I heard the sound of his guitar as he played *Amazing Grace*. Tears flowed and flowed!

Remember I was asked in the beginning of this whole event by whose authority did I say those words, *In the name of Jesus Christ you are healed?* Surely not mine but by His authority and power given to me, His daughter, by the sacrifice He made for me and us all. Spiritual authority is activated by faith. And you have the same authority and power.

Spiritual Warfare

> *For our struggle is not against flesh and blood, but against the rulers, against the authorities, against the powers of this dark world and against spiritual forces of evil in the heavenly realms (Ephesians 6:12, NIV)*

What is spiritual warfare? It is the act of joining God in the battle against Satan and his evil forces (demons) in the heavenly realms. In Revelation 12 an account is given about how Satan, known then as Lucifer, rebelled in heaven and was cast down from heaven to earth because of his pride – he wanted to be like God and to be worshipped as God. With him came one third of the angels to rebel with him; these are called demons, (see Revelation 12:7-17). Satan which means *'accuser'* in Hebrew is constantly accusing and harassing God's people. His purpose is to destroy us.

> *Your enemy the devil prowls around like a roaring lion looking for someone to devour.*
> **(1 Peter 5: 8b, NIV.**

> *The thief comes only to steal and kill and destroy*
> **(John 10:10, NIV).**

> *He (Satan) was a murderer from the beginning, not holding to the truth, for there is no truth in him. When he lies, he speaks his native language, for he is a liar and the father of lies.*
> **(John 8: 44b, NIV)**

Our first offensive move is taking Jesus as our Lord and Savior. At that moment we are marked as His own and the enemy is given notice that we belong to the Lord. From that moment on, there is a spiritual battle for our souls. We know that the battle has already been won at the cross. *And having disarmed the powers and authorities, he made a public spectacle of them, triumphing over them by the Cross.* (Colossians 2:15, NIV)

So if the battle has already been won, why are we fighting? Yes, the battle has been won in the heavenly realms, but Satan still has power on this earth until Jesus returns. We still have our *'flesh'*, our unsurrendered soul, which has not yet fully submitted to God. Unhealed hurts and unmet needs still need to be healed. We are called to work out our *salvation in fear and trembling* (Philippians 2:12) for we are on a journey of dying to *'self'* and living to Christ becoming more infused with the character of God daily which brings with it a greater power and authority through Jesus Christ.

Legal Ground of Satan

Legal ground refers to those areas in our lives where we are linked to evil or deception either knowingly or without our knowledge. Legal ground includes the following:

- Bitterness and bitter root judgements
- Cult involvement of self or ancestors
- Generational ties and/or inherited curses
- Inner vows or slogans
- Spiritual adultery
- Wrong soul ties (psychological, sexual)

Demonic weapons are fear, doubt, and deception. Without these weapons the enemy is powerless against the resurrection truth of Jesus Christ. We, as His followers, need to recognize the above weapons at work in us then bring the work of Christ to heal the root causes of these lies. God's truth sets us free and then we come to know our authority in Him.

In the *Episcopal Book of Common Prayer* the following questions are asked at baptism: (page 302):

> *Question*   Do you renounce Satan and all the spiritual forces of wickedness that rebel against God?
> *Answer*   I renounce them.
> *Question*   Do you renounce the evil powers of this world which corrupt and destroy the creatures of God?
> *Answer*   I renounce them.
> *Question*   Do you renounce all sinful desires that draw you from the love of God?
> *Answer*   I renounce them.

Christians are vulnerable to spiritual attack by Satan when a demon has legal entry by a wrong belief, distortion of truth or lie we believe and/ or our own willful choice. Sins of the flesh are open gates for demonic harassment and oppression.

- Unrighteous anger
- Greed/ covetousness
- Jealousy/ envy
- Lust
- Gluttony
- Gossip
- Strife
- Bitterness
- Self-Righteousness
- Criticizing, blaming, judging
- Unforgiveness
- Addictions (alcohol, drugs, food, and other substances- compulsive behaviors or behaviors that become compulsive like shopping, gambling, sex, work, housework, religious distraction for the sake of medicating feelings, exercise.

Bitter Root Judgments

See to it that no root of bitterness springing up causes trouble, and by it many be defiled.

(Hebrews 12:15)

Do not judge lest you be judged yourselves. For in the way you judge, you will be judged; and by your standard of measure, it shall be measured to you.

(Matthew 7:1-2)

Bitter root judgments are our fleshly or sinful way of responding to negative events that have happened to us in our lives. We are reminded by God to not judge for it will come back on us yet that is exactly what we do to those who have harmed us or even others we love. *Therefore, there is now no condemnation for those who are in Christ Jesus,* (Romans 8:1, ESV) and yet we condemn. When we bitterly judge another, we refuse to forgive them for the wrong they have done. Forgiveness is a command. *Forgive us our debts as we also have forgiven our debtors,* (Matthew 6:12 ESV). We don't forgive and we will reap unforgiveness. We condemn and judge others and it will be returned to us. This is an unchangeable law of God: We reap what we sow.

Where do Bitter Root judgments start? Many times the root can be found in our families of origin. We all have judged our parents somewhere along the line in our lives. I judged my biological alcoholic father by making the inner vow *I will never be like my father.* It sounded good at the time, but I judged his character and God does not give me that right to judge him. I still must honor his position as my biological father though I do not have to honor or approve of his behavior. So, we judge our parents and our siblings for the hurts we received from them and even the unmet needs that they failed to provide us with while we were growing up.

One of the most difficult abuses to deal with are the cases of child sexual abuse, especially when it is a family member. "I cannot forgive him after what he did to me" she cried as the pain of that abuse spilled out of her wounded heart and body. "And no one believed me," she said. Healing takes time and this case has needed to take that time. The healing and the forgiveness happen layer by layer as she trusts God more and more. Yes she can certainly judge the behavior of that family member but she can't by God's law judge the motivation or the heart of this perpetrator. It's God's job.

If we judge another's motivation or heart, we plant a seed of bitter root judgment in our own hearts and it will grow bitterly inside us. It acts like a curse in our lives and will bring to pass in our own life what we are judging in another. It becomes a prison in us. Remember in chapter 6 the story of the angry man in Hospice who was one of my clients during my internship as part of the Masters in Psychology work? He had judged his father's character and heart when he was punished for a deed he didn't do. That bitter root judgment planted in his own heart at age fifteen remained and grew in his life until finally, at age eighty-two he forgave his father. All those years he became embittered with life and his wife received the brunt of that bitterness.

The following is an example of bitter root expectancy taken from Elishasmantle.com (accessed October 25, 2016)

> *A man is brought up by a critical mother, he, feeling wounded and rejected, learns to protect his heart by withdrawing from her. His experiences with mother form a picture of 'women'. When he marries, he fears pain and vulnerability and consciously (or unconsciously) projects his expectations onto his wife, holding her at a distance. She is lonely and appeals to him to share with her. He interprets this as criticism (whether it is or not) and pulls farther away. He criticizes her attempts to break through the walls of his heart.* (Elishasmantle.com, 2014)

Many of us know we need to forgive but we don't look deeper to see if we have judged that one we have forgiven. We will know by the fruit in our lives. If we are bitter and easily condemn others or have negative expectations in life, we can be assured we have sown bitter root judgements from past wounding events in our lives. Ask the Holy Spirit to reveal to you any bitter root judgements that are hidden in your heart. Look at the following pattern of bitter judgement:

If our spouses have changed and they are not like they were before we married them, it may very well be that they have been defiled by our judging. (A Path to Freedom, internet, accessed Oct 25, 2016)

There is a pattern:
- a) Alcoholic father, alcoholic husband
- b) Poor providing parent, poor providing husband
- c) Weak father, weak husband
- d) Cold and distant father, cold and distant spouse
- e) Critical parent, critical spouse
- f) Workaholic father, workaholic husband
- g) Sick mother, sick wife
- h) Rejecting father, rejecting spouse
- i) Unfaithful father, unfaithful spouse
- j) Abusive father, abusive husband
- k) Absent father, absent spouse

(A Path to Freedom, internet, accessed Oct 25, 2016)

What do we do with these bitter root judgements living and operating inside us and how do we break these negative patterns? I encourage you right now to stop and examine your heart. Who are you still judging? Who haven't you forgiven? What wounded event from your past keeps running through your mind? Recognize the roots of these bitter judgements. Be aware of the negative fruit in your life. Ask the Holy Spirit to take you to this root when the bitter judgment began. See or know by faith Jesus is right there with you when this occurred. He is always with you. See the one who harmed you and watch Jesus with that one. Repent of your bitter judgment on that person. When you are ready standing right there with Jesus, speak forgiveness to the one who hurt you or didn't nurture you. Pray aloud:

I forgive you. What you did was wrong, you hurt me. (Be specific). But I release you from my judgment and you are set free to Jesus and so am I. Lord forgive me for keeping this pattern going on in my life and for wounding my own spouse, children, etc.

All these bitter root judgements and negative expectations are at the foot of the cross now covered by the blood of Jesus Christ who forgives all your sins.

If you forgive anyone's sins, their sins are forgiven; if you do not forgive them, they are not forgiven. (John 20:23).

Powers of the Dark World

What is the Occult?

Occult is, *that which is hidden, secret or concealed; matters involving the supernatural.* (Webster's New Collegiate Dictionary, 2014). Occult refers to the practice of dealings with the world of spirits or spiritual forces other than the Triune Godhead: Father, Son and Holy Spirit. Examples of occult practices: fortune telling, magic practices, Spiritism, and psychic phenomenon.

What is a Cult?

Cults teach some other way than Jesus to salvation (John 14:6) and believe that salvation comes through keeping the teaching of the cult, not through the Messiah, Jesus Christ of Nazareth. Cults also may teach that Jesus did not come in the flesh (1 John 4:1-2).

Many cults are involved in *'hidden'* knowledge and supremacy of the human being. The word cult means that which is hidden or secret. It signifies participation or involvement in the spiritual world in order to gain knowledge or power, often to do evil. Leaders of cults often have charismatic personalities.

Characteristics of Cults:

- Use psychological coercion to recruit, indoctrinate, and retain members
- Form elitist society
- Founder is self-appointed, dogmatic, messianic, not accountable, and has charisma
- Believes the end justifies the means
- Its wealth does not benefit its members or society.

Examples of Cults:

- Christian Scientist
- Mormon or Latter Day Saints
- Jehovah's Witnesses
- Unitarianism
- Universalism
- Scientology

Our Defense

Armor of God

Finally, be strong in the Lord and in his mighty power. Put on the full armor of God so that you can take your stand against the devils schemes. For our struggle is not against flesh and blood, but against the rulers, against the authorities, against the powers of this dark world and against the spiritual forces of evil in the heavenly realms. Therefore put on the full armor of God, so that when the day of evil comes, you may be able to stand your ground, and after you have done everything, to stand. Stand firm then, with the belt of truth buckled around your waist, with the breastplate of righteousness in place, and with your feet fitted with the readiness that comes from the gospel of peace. In addition to all this, take up the shield of faith, with which you can extinguish all flaming arrows of the evil one. Take the helmet of salvation and the sword of the Spirit, which is the word of God. And pray in the Spirit on all occasions with all kinds of prayer and requests. (Ephesians 6:10-18, NIV)

God has provided us with all the armor we need as soldiers in His army. The armor is the very living character of God! We are covered from head to toe with Jesus himself. *But put on the Lord Jesus Christ and make no provision for the flesh to fulfill its lusts.* (Romans 13:14 NKJV). For each part of the armor is an aspect of Jesus' character/nature: truth, righteousness, peace, faith, salvation, word of God, and Spirit. A revelation came to me as I was putting on the armor of God one day in preparation for a conference. Suddenly the armor came alive. I do not know how to describe this, but every part of the armor is living and breathing...alive. Putting on Christ is real.

Our adversary, Satan the devil, will come against us again and again and trying to break down our mental resistance and take our mind and emotions captive. The battleground is in the soul that houses our mind, will, and emotions! The Word of God states:

Submit yourselves then, to God. Resist the devil, and he will flee from you.
(James 4:7, NIV).

We are warned to

Be self-controlled and alert. Your enemy the devil prowls around like a roaring lion looking for someone to devour.
(1 Peter 5:5, NIV).

Satan may attack, oppress and harass us, but he can only gain ground where we let him in through on open door. What open door? A chink in our armor refers to the area of vulnerability or weak spot in a suit of armor. Our sins knowingly or unknowingly are vulnerable areas in our unsurrendered, uncrucified souls.

We defend ourselves with the shield of faith and the offensive weapon, the Word of God. With the shield of faith, we extinguish the arrows of lust, jealousy, doubt, guilt, and all other kinds of temptations. By the sword of the Spirit, God's Word, we overcome the evil one by God's truth exposing the lies of Satan, breaking generational bondages, as we are set free.

Deliverance Prayer

Deliverance is the action of being rescued or set free. God rescues His people from their enemies (1 Samuel 17:37) and delivers us from ourselves and the very perils of sin that ensnare us. (Galatians 1:4; Colossians 1:13; Romans 4:25; 1Thessalonians 1:10).

Deliverance prayer is another weapon God has given us for spiritual warfare. Deliverance prayer refers to the form of prayer whereby 'spirits or demons' are named and "cast off" of the person being prayed for by the authority of Jesus Christ in those who are praying. The individual being prayed for renounces these spirits of darkness in deliverance prayer, through Christ's authority.

And these signs will accompany those who believe: in My name they will drive out demons...

(Mark 16:17a, NIV)

Evil spirits (demons) must bow to the Name of Jesus.

With authority and power He gives orders to evil spirits and they come out.

(Luke 4: 36b, NIV)

He called His twelve disciples to Him and gave them authority to drive out evil spirits and to heal every disease and sickness.

(Matthew 10:1, NIV)

Christians can be harassed by Satan and his demons, but this is not *'possession'* by an evil spirit. Only non-Christians (anyone who has not accepted Jesus Christ as Lord and Savior) can be possessed. Exorcism is praying for non-Christians to be set free from evil spirits. Deliverance prayer is for Christians who may need help when they are experiencing in their souls oppression, depression, obsession, addiction, and other more serious spiritual issues. These negative spirits may have been given *legal ground* due to an involvement with a cult or occult or through unrepented, repeated sin generationally or oneself, or through the wounds others have inflicted on you. Through the authority and power of Jesus Christ we can do deliverance prayer delivering us from the evil spirits and their influence. However, it is often much more beneficial to begin with inner healing prayer rather than deliverance prayer. Inner healing prayer takes back the legal ground that Satan had temporarily obtained. As each unhealed hurt and unmet need is healed the demonic spirits have less and less to hold onto and deliverance prayer becomes much easier.

Some types of deliverance prayer:

- Renouncing the influence of cult involvement
- Renouncing the influence of occult involvement
- Breaking wrong soul ties (sexual, soul, etc.)
- Breaking inner vows or word curses
- Renouncing compulsive, immoral sexual activity
- Renouncing addictive behaviors
- Renouncing specific evil spirits (i.e. fear, anxiety, disease, judgment, rage, perversion, pride, torment, depression, lying, etc.)

Summation: Victory in Jesus

Through all these things we are more than conquerors through him who loved us,

(Romans 8:37).

Yes, we are in a battle here on this earth. It is a battle for our souls. How do we enter the battle with full confidence of victory?

- Repent of our sins and turn from them
- Receive inner healing and deliverance prayer in our souls
- Receive and give forgiveness and receive cleansing through the Blood of Jesus Christ
- Walk in truth and love in the authority of Jesus Christ
- Reconcile with others when possible proclaiming the word of God

A daily prescription of reading and inwardly digesting God's Word will help keep the enemy at bay even though he still tries to attack us. Sitting in God's Presence and worshipping Him girds up our spiritual immune system. Putting on the very character of Christ, our living armor, has us ready to walk out the door in full confidence in God. *For the battle is not yours but God's,* (2 Chronicles 20:15). Proclaim His word in boldness to others.

Chapter 8
WHERE'S THE POWER?

The dilemma many of us feel in our lives is that we do not have power. I mean have you ever tried to change someone? I love to ask that question of spouses. They always laugh! We can't even change ourselves. We need power! *The Big Book of Alcoholics Anonymous* states: *...lack of power was our dilemma* (p 45)

When I was baptized as a two-year-old in the name of the Father, Son and Holy Spirit I received all of God yet somehow, I didn't have the key to turn on the power. As I aged, I relied more on my own power. I was a striver! I experienced successes, especially professionally, but I couldn't conquer my negative responses to offense and rejection. I discovered that I have no power to change anything, to do anything. Can you relate? We are following Christ, yet there is still chaos in our lives, storms going on in our families, and battles raging at work. God's Word states:

> *...be self-controlled and alert. Your enemy the devil prowls around like a roaring lion looking for someone to devour. Resist him, standing firm in the faith, because you know that your brothers throughout the world are undergoing the same kind of sufferings*
>
> (1 Peter 5:8-9).

Have you tried to resist the devil on your own? You will get beat up! We know what is missing – power, but how do we get it?

I sent a young man in a church where I was serving as assistant priest, to a renewal weekend. The weekend transformed his life. He met Jesus! His wife didn't know him when he returned home. Who is this man that is kneeling next to his bed saying prayers at night and asking me to join him? Shortly after that weekend, he came bursting into my office demanding, "I know there is more to this and I know you know. Whatever it is I want it!" After gathering my wits about me, I began to tell him about the Holy Spirit. You see he knew he was missing power in his life. There were things he was still doing, like smoking pot, drinking, and chewing tobacco that didn't line up with God but he didn't know how to change that. Somehow, he hadn't tapped into the power source in God which he needed in order to live the Christian life fully.

Yes, he had met Jesus Christ powerfully and had given his life to Him. Born again means we have a new nature in Christ. However, we still have a sin nature within that resists this new nature in us. Not everything in us has been healed just because we turn our lives over to Christ. The work of the cross must be applied to the wounded, unhealed sin areas in our souls. Our old behavior will try to draw us back into old sinful behavior over and over until we are healed of the root of this sinful behavior. This sin nature problem is a problem for all Christians.

Listen to St Paul:

> *I know that nothing good lives in me, that is, in my sinful nature. For I have the desire to do what is good, but I cannot carry it out. For what I do is not the good I want to do; no, the evil I do not want to do—this I keep on doing. Now if I do what I do not want to do, it is no longer I who do it, but it is sin living in me that does it*
>
> (Rom. 7:18-20).

We understand this dilemma. Again reiterating the theologian Karl Barth, (1982), this is the battle between the *'yes'* of God and the *'no'* of our human nature. Paul summarizes this discourse with a conclusion:

> *What a wretched man I am! Who will rescue me from this body of death? Thanks be to God—through Jesus Christ our Lord!*
> **(Rom. 7:24-25).**

We too discover that we still cannot solve our own problems even after we are saved. Paul even though humbled by his human sinful nature knew about power! He had been baptized by the power of the Holy Spirit that comes through the Father and the Son. This is the baptism that John the Baptist speaks about.

> *I baptize you with water for repentance, but he who is coming after me is mightier than I, whose sandals I am not worthy to carry. He will baptize you with the Holy Spirit and fire,*
> **(Matthew 3:11).**

So this young man stood before me demanding that I share all that God has for us with him! So I prayed and he asked the Holy Spirit to fill him and give him the gifts of the Holy Spirit. Suddenly he was filled with a warmth, a fire that began to burn within his heart. He began to speak in tongues of angels which Paul alludes to in 1 Cor 13:1 …*if I speak in the tongues of men and of angels*… He left my office so filled with joy! Today he is a worship leader and a prayer facilitator in the inner healing ministry.

The Power of the Holy Spirit

But you shall receive power when the Holy Spirit has come upon you; and you shall be witnesses to Me in Jerusalem, and in all Judea and Samaria, and to the end of the earth. (Acts 1:8, NKJ).

The Greek word for *'receive'* means to take hold of, to catch, to obtain, to take as one's own and to be amazed. Since we were baptized into the name of the Father, Son and Holy Spirt, we received the Holy Spirit but had it been released in us? In the Anglican/Episcopal church when a young person is confirmed around age thirteen or so the Bishop sometimes give you a slight slap across the cheek indicating and confirming the Holy Spirit is now manifest in you. I understand a few bishops were more heavy-handed than others in this ritual! Who is the Holy Spirit?

Person of the Holy Spirit

Who is the Holy Spirit? The Third person of the Trinity, who exercises the power of the Father and the Son in creation and redemption is the Holy Spirit. The Holy Spirit lives in us and is the power by which believers come to Christ and helps us overcome our human inadequacy. Through the Holy Spirit we see with new eyes of faith, He is closer to us than we are to ourselves. The Holy Spirit is the one through whom all else is seen in a new light. It is through the eyes of the Holy Spirit that the Father–Son relationship is viewed. The secret of drawing on the power of the Holy Spirit is faith.

The Holy Spirit has the characteristics of a Person:

1) He has the human characteristics of mind (Romans 8:27), will (1 Corinthians 12:11), and feeling (Ephesians 4:30)
2) His activities are many: enlightening (2Pet 1:21), teaching (John 14:26), witnessing (Hebrews 10:15), interceding (Romans 8:26),

speaking (Revelation 2:7), commanding (Acts 16: 6, 7), and testifying (John 15:26).
3) He has relationship with human beings: He can be grieved (Ephesians 4:30), lied to (Acts 5:3), and blasphemed (Matthew 12:31, 32)
4) He has the divine characteristics of the Godhead: eternal (Hebrews 9:14), omnipresent (Psalm 139: 7-10), omnipotent (Luke 1:35), and omniscient (1 Corinthians 2: 10, 11)
5) He has several names in scripture: Spirit of God, the Spirit of Christ, the Comforter, the Holy Spirit, the Holy Spirit of promise, the Spirit of truth, the Spirit of grace, the Spirit of life, the Spirit of adoption, and the Spirit of holiness. His presence is demonstrated by: fire (Acts 2:1, 2), wind (Acts 2:1, 2), water (John 7: 37-39), a seal (Ephesians 1:3), oil (Acts 10:38), a dove (John 1:32).

As Christians we need to realize that within us is the fullness of the Godhead. The omnipotence of God lives in us and that there is no problem, no dilemma that God cannot solve. It is through faith relying on the Holy Spirit daily in our walk with God. The Holy Spirit's attitude and ministry are marked by generosity. His chief purpose is to illumine Jesus' teaching, to glorify the person of Jesus Christ, to bring comfort and encouragement and to work in the life of the individual believer and the church.

The Holy Spirit is present all through Scripture. In the Old Testament He hovers over the waters in creation (Genesis 1). The Holy Spirit anointed Old Testament prophets to prophecy and to write (Joel, Isaiah). God's word prophesied that the Holy Spirit would be poured out and His gifts exercised in the Church (Joel 2: 28-32; Acts 2: 17-21). Also read Isaiah 28: 11, 12, then 1 Corinthians 14: 21, 22 and Acts 2: 1-11; 10:45, 46 for deeper understanding of the work of the Holy Spirit.

In the New Testament, Jesus refers to the Spirit of God (Matthew 12:28–29; Luke 11:20) as the power by which He is casting out demons, and invading the stronghold of Beelzebub and freeing those held captive. After Jesus was baptized by John in the Jordon river the Holy Spirit came down in bodily form like a dove on Him (Luke 3:22). The dove is a symbol of purity and demonstrates that Jesus is endowed with holiness and innocence. Also the dove refers back to the account of the flood and Noah's ark. Noah sent out a dove several times and on the last flight he brought back an olive branch, which is symbolic of peace, (Genesis 8:11). Likewise God declares peace on all of mankind. Now at Jesus' baptism, again the dove brings the good news of reconciliation of God with mankind. The kingdom of God is being ushered in and the Holy Spirit works with the Father and Son in realizing the redeeming power of the kingdom of God. God's kingdom is not only the reign of the Son but also the reign of the Spirit, as all share in the reign of the Father.

The person and ministry of the Holy Spirit in the Gospels is confirmed by His work in the early church. The baptism with the Holy Spirit (Acts 1:5) is the pouring out of the Spirit's power in missions and evangelism (Acts 1:8). This prophecy of Jesus (and of Joel 2:28-32) begins on Pentecost (Acts 2:1-18). Many of those who hear of the finished work of God in Jesus' death and resurrection (Acts 2:32-38) repent of their sins. In this act of repentance, they receive the gift of the Holy Spirit (Acts 2:38), becoming witnesses of God's grace through the Spirit. The Holy Spirit is given as a gift to the church to guarantee that the continued ministry of the resurrected Christ is both communicated and corroborated. The Holy Spirit is the expressed power of the Trinity.

Understanding who the Holy Sprit is and the work of the Holy Spirit is critical to inner healing prayer work. We have no power ourselves for healing another or ourselves of unhealed hurts, unmet needs and unresolved issues, but the Holy Spirit who dwells in us does have that power to liberate all of us who are held captive by these negative events in our lives, past or present. In Paul's letters he states that Christian liberty stems from the work of the Holy Spirit:

Where the Spirit of the Lord is, there is liberty (2 Cor. 3:17). This is a process of beholding as in a mirror the glory of the Lord, and being transformed into the same image from glory to glory, just as by the Spirit of the Lord

(2 Cor. 3:18).

The personal work of the Holy Spirit is accordingly one with that of the Father and the Son, so Paul can relate the grace, love, and communion of The Trinity in a Trinitarian benediction: *The grace of the Lord Jesus Christ, and the love of God, and the communion of the Holy Spirit be with you all. Amen* (2 Cor. 13:14).

Receive Power

After Jesus' resurrection and before His ascension He appeared to the disciples. The first thing He said was *Peace be with you*, (John 20:19). Then after He showed them His hands and side He again repeated *Peace be with you*, and declared their mission: *as the Father has sent me, I am sending you,* (John 20:21). Jesus Christ, the incarnate Son of God, who is the Prince of peace, speaks peace into them. That peace is incarnated in them through the Word Himself. That is the first step. He verifies that it is Him by the witness of His crucifixion wounds. He commissions them to go out into this world just like He did. *...proclaim the Gospel... baptize... cast out demons...lay hands on the sick and they will recover* (Mark 16:15-18). But where's the power? How are we going to do this? Isn't that the question we still ask? *And with that he breathed on them and said, 'Receive the Holy Spirit,'* (John 20:22).

He breathed on them. The Greek word used here, *emphysao*, and according to the *Blue Letter Bible Lexicon*, is used nowhere else in the New Testament but it is the one used by the Septuagint translators of Genesis 2:7. *And the Lord God formed man of the dust of the ground, and breathed into his nostrils the breath of life;* and man became a living soul.

In Genesis God's creation of man is completed and now as written in the Gospel of John on the day of Jesus' resurrection a new creation has begun. The root of the Greek word *'breathe'* means to beget, to bring forth, to produce, to spring up and to be born. The very breath of God begets us as His children, His offspring. We are born again and adopted as His children through Christ.

Power Comes Upon You

The Holy Spirit was breathed on the disciples but they had not yet received it.

> *But you shall receive power when the Holy Spirit has come upon you; and you shall be witnesses to Me in Jerusalem, and in all Judea and Samaria, and to the end of the earth.*
>
> **(Acts 1:8, NKJ).**

Another movement of the Holy Spirit must happen before the power is released in and through them. They will receive power when the Holy Spirit comes upon them. The Greek word for receive, *lambano*, means to take in, to get hold of and to accept.

What were the disciples taking in, getting hold of? Power! The Greek word for power is *Dunamis* meaning force, the miraculous, the ability of God's mighty work operating in them to become His vessels of divine healing and works. They received this dynamite power of God when the Holy Spirit supervened upon them on behalf of God Himself. At that divine moment Jesus proclaims that it will now come to pass that they have become and are becoming His witnesses, His martyrs of the Gospel of Jesus Christ for the sake of Christ. They are now on record so to speak. They are new creations.

Power Overshadows You

And the angel answered and said to her, "The Holy Spirit will come upon you, and the power of the Highest will overshadow you; therefore, also, that Holy One who is to be born will be called the Son of God. (Luke 1:35 NKJ)

The power of the Highest actually overshadows us when it comes upon us. By analogy it means to envelop us, like Mary, in a haze of brilliancy. We, like her, are invested with an extraordinary influence. Mary, so highly favored among women births in the flesh, the Son of God. Now us, becoming highly favored through the death and resurrection of our Lord and Savior, now receive Jesus into us through the Holy Spirit and we are born again to carry His presence throughout the whole earth. Jesus Christ through the empowerment of the Holy Spirit develops and grows in you and me.

At the completion of teaching on the Holy Spirit at our healing conference I invited all the participants to come forward and ask the Holy Spirit to be released in you. I asked our team to come and stand behind praying for all the people who came forward, but not to touch them. Suddenly, a man started to shake. The Holy Spirit was working on and in him. I found out he was from a halfway house and he was detoxed right there on the spot! Others began to speak in tongues and some began to dance in the spirit. It was beautiful to watch. The joy of the Lord breaking out. His power and love overshadowing us!

Power Endues You

Behold, I send the Promise of My Father upon you; but tarry in the city of Jerusalem until you are endued with power from on high. (Luke 24:49 NKJ).

All God's promise are *'yes'* and *'amen'*, (2 Corinthians 1:20). It is not only an announcement from God but a pledge of His divine assurance of good. The Holy Spirit is God's promise, God's pledge that is ours for the asking. He tells the disciples to tarry in Jerusalem, to stay right at home until they are endued with this power from Him. Don't move, be steadfast and the promise will come. To be endued is to be invested, to be girded about with every garment of God, His robe of righteousness, His character traits. The word endued carries a sense of sinking down into a garment, being so enfolded with it as to be wrapped up in it. This is how His dynamite floods into us. Why? To be witnesses that it was necessary for Christ to suffer and die and to rise from the dead on the third day and that repentance and remission of sins should be preached in His name to all nations beginning in Jerusalem. We can only do this through the power of the Holy Spirit.

Power Unites Us

Now when the Day of Pentecost had fully come, they were all with one accord in one place. And suddenly there came a sound from heaven, as of a rushing mighty wind, and it filled the whole house where they were sitting. Then there appeared to them divided tongues, as of fire, and one sat upon each of them. And they were all filled with the Holy Spirit and began to speak with other tongues, as the Spirit gave them utterance.
(Acts 2:1-4 NKJ)

... they were all with one accord in one place. Have you ever tried to get your vestry or deacons' board to agree on what color the church should be painted? The Holy Spirit unites us, bringing us into one mind, with one accord, with one passion. Inner healing works like this. For example a person has had a tragedy happen in his/her life. The evil one thrusts

everything he can to make that person bitter, or depressed or just want to give up on life. But that is not God's design or plan for that person. *For I know the thoughts that I think toward you, says the LORD, thoughts of peace and not of evil, to give you a future and a hope,* (Jeremiah 29:11 NKJV). As we pray through the tragic event, Jesus manifests Himself in some way showing the person that He was there all along, He never left. Lie after lie of the enemy is broken by Jesus' manifest truth and love. The person's mind, will and emotions are brought into unity with God's mind, will and emotions as the healing happens. The tragic event occurred but it is now viewed through Jesus which changes everything. Forgiveness and freedom flow and the person is set free now that he/she is in one accord with God.

This unique Greek word for one accord, *homothumadon*, is a compound of two words meaning to '*rush along*' and 'in *unison*'. It makes me think of a musical composition. Have you ever heard people singing together in the spirit? The Holy Spirit is giving different notes, different harmonies, tones and even different rhythms to people and together it is glorious. All directed by the conductor, the Holy Spirit. This occurred recently at an Episcopal Church during our Healing School Level 1 conference. At the end of singing a worship song, the Spirit led us to keep singing but it was a new song. People who had never experienced that in their whole lives were wonderfully stunned and participated fully. One older woman explained, "I thought I was in heaven! It was so wonderful! The Holy Spirt blends together the lives of all of us in Christ's Church.

On the Day of Pentecost, this sound like a rushing wind came as they were all together in a room, of one mind. Each one was filled, literally much like cramming a net to over filling with fish. Each one was satisfied and fulfilled as the Holy Spirit came upon them. There appeared something like tongues of fire resting upon each disciple's head. All were favored. Why did this happen? To fulfill Christ's prophecy:

> *Now I am no longer in the world, but these are in the world, and I come to You. Holy Father, keep through Your name those whom You have given Me, that they may be one as We are.*
>
> (John 17:11 (NKJ)

The disciples poured out of that room no longer fearful but filled with the Holy Spirit and each began to speak in other languages, languages they had not previously learned. This still happens today. I have had this incredible experience happen three times with Spanish. Believe me, my Spanish is very limited!

I sat in the small room provided for me at the Language Institute for Missionaries, Costa Rica, waiting for the next prayer appointment. A lovely young Spanish woman walked in with a little boy about four years old clinging to her. She explained to my translator that for the past six months he wouldn't walk anywhere or be without his mother. She had to carry him everywhere and he gave her no explanation. No one knew what to do. Something has happened to this little boy to frighten him so but we didn't know what.

I prayed asking for the blood of Jesus to cover us all in this prayer time and asking the Holy Spirit to guide us and take us to the root of this terrible fear gripping this boy. I continued praying in English as my translator shared my words in Spanish to the mother and the boy. He was clinging to his mother even more. Suddenly my language changed though at the time I thought I was speaking in tongues, the angelic kind. My translator stopped speaking, looking at me with a surprised look on her face. While continuing to speak in this tongue, I watched this little boy let go of his mother and sit alongside of her at peace. The grin on his face told me the healing that Jesus had done. The mother jumped up, gave me a hug, saying *Gracias! Gracias! Gloria Dios!* and ran excitedly out the door with her boy in tow.

My translator looked at me and said, "I thought you didn't speak Spanish"

"I don't!" I replied as stunned as she was. With little time to discuss what happened, in walked the next prayer appointment. To this day I don't know what happened, but I do know that God happened even if I don't know the details! I would love to tell you that I have that gift of Spanish all the time. It has only come when God sends it for a specific time, person and place. This gift of language put the mother, the boy, the translator and I all in unity with God and healing happened. His gifts truly unify us.

A. W. Tozer speaks about unity in this way:

> *Has it ever occurred to you that one hundred pianos all tuned to the same fork are automatically tuned to each other? They are of one accord by being tuned, not to each other, but to another standard to which each one must individually bow. So one hundred worshippers meeting together, each one looking away to Christ, are in heart nearer to each other than they could possibly be were they to become 'unity' conscious and turn their eyes away from God to strive for closer fellowship. The body becomes stronger as its members become healthier.* (Tozer, 2019)

Empowerment of the Holy Spirit brings the fire of God to our hearts stirring up His passion in us. Jim Elliot missionary to the tribes in Ecuador said: He makes His ministers a flame of fire. Am I ignitable? God deliver me from the dread asbestos of 'other things.' Saturate me with the oil of the Spirit that I may be aflame. But flame is transient, often short lived. Canst thou bear this, my soul - short life? ... Make me thy fuel, Flame of God. (Elliot, 2013). Jim Elliot was an evangelical Christian who was one of the missionaries killed while attempting to evangelize the Huaorani people of Ecuador. The native who killed Jim Elliot, later repented, turning his life over to Christ. He became a powerful preacher in Ecuador.

Be Filled

Paul writes in Ephesians *"Be filled with the Spirit"* (Eph. 5:18). The word *'be filled'* is in the present tense and indicates that this blessing is one we can continuously experience and enjoy now. It is also a command which seems to not leave an option for a responsive disciple of Christ. Finally these words are in the passive voice which means being filled with the Spirit is not something we can achieve through our own efforts but is something that is done for us and to us in which we submit. What a beautiful scripture that depicts a loving theocentric view of the Holy Spirit's filling. Our God reaches down to gather us up into ultimate communion with Him.

Gifts

Each member of the Godhead plays a role in giving gifts to mankind. Our existence—human life—is given by the Father (Gen. 2:7; Heb. 12:9), who also gave His only begotten Son as the Redeemer for humanity (John 3:16). Our redemption is from Jesus, the giver of eternal life (John 5:38–40; 10:27, 28). He gave His life and shed His blood to redeem us from our sin, (John 10:17, 18; Eph. 5:25–27). The Holy Spirit who proceeds from the Father and Son has been sent to us (Acts 2:17, 33) to advance the work of redemption through the church's ministry of worship, growth, healing, and evangelism.

Release of the Holy Spirit within You

(1) First you must be born again. You belong to Jesus and have the indwelling Spirit. *You, however, are controlled not by the sinful nature but by the Spirit, if the Spirit of God lives in you. And if anyone does not have the Spirit of Christ, he does not belong to Christ.* (Romans 8:9 NIV)

(2) You have to ask. Ask for the Holy Spirit and your prayer will be answered. *I tell you, though he will not get up and give him the bread because he is his friend, yet because of the man's boldness he will get up and give him as much as he needs. So I say to you: Ask and it will be given to you; seek and you will find; knock and the door will be opened to you. For everyone who asks receives; he who seeks finds; and to him who knocks, the door will be opened.* (Luke 11:8 NIV)

(3) You have to surrender. "Present your bodies a living sacrifice. *Therefore, I urge you, brothers, in view of God's mercy, to offer your bodies as living sacrifices, holy and pleasing to God-- this is your spiritual act of worship."* (Romans 12:1 NIV)

(4) You must be willing to obey the Holy Spirit. You can't pick and choose what not to obey. *"And we are His witnesses to these things, and so also is the Holy Spirit whom God has given to those who obey Him."* (Acts 5:32 NKJ)

(5) You need to believe. *I would like to learn just one thing from you: Did you receive the Spirit by observing the law, or by believing what you heard?* ((Galatians 3:2NIV)

(6) You have to exercise what God has given you. You need to respond to what you have been given by faith. *"… they began to speak with other tongues as the as the Spirit gave them utterance"* (Acts 2:4 NIV). They spoke the words the Spirit gave them. The Holy Spirit gave the words and they voluntarily responded. Their response was based on faith. You need only to reach out and take it.

I sat across the dining room table from my friends whom I had met at Cursillo, a renewal retreat put on by the Episcopal Church. The wife was on the team. Jesus met me in a most powerful way on that weekend. At one point during the retreat the spiritual director said: "Meet Jesus now!" I turned around and the wife of this couple was standing behind me and I saw Jesus in her face.

"I see Jesus!" I exclaimed.

She responded, "Where?"

I exclaimed, "In your face!"

"In my face!" she yelled with her eyes wide open.

"Yes, in your face!" And as I looked around, I could see Him in many faces.

One glance from Christ at that retreat and glorious joy through copious tears became mine with just His deep internal invitation to meet Him now. I am forever changed.

After Cursillo this couple invited me to spend Easter with them while my son was visiting his father. Great idea because I had questions for them, lots of them. Lately the Lord had led me to read Acts 2. When you first read that what did you think? I was flabbergasted! Tongues of fire? Wind rushing through? Sounds of heaven? Speaking in other tongues? What is this? So I turned to my new female friend and asked her about speaking in tongues: "Do you do that?" She nodded yes. Well that sort of floored me. Quickly turning to her husband who I thought must be very wise since he had a beard, I asked him, "Do you do that speaking in tongues stuff?" I was not exactly theological in my questioning. He nodded yes. Well there you have it. "How do you get it?" I asked.

Such a simple answer they offered, "You ask the Holy Spirit for it." So since I was convinced you could only get these gifts from God in church, I explained I would ask for it at the end of the Wednesday night service at their little store front Episcopal church.

The service ended and my friend came back asking me if I was ready. Part of me was scared to death. I walked up to the altar and knelt down. I was sure I needed to do that to receive this strange gift. My friend knelt beside me. Immediately I hear a lovely cacophony of voices in the most beautiful love languages I'd ever heard. Behind me stood a group of about five or six people who were praying in tongues simultaneously. After listening for a while my friend poked me and said, "You have to ask for the Holy Spirit to fill you and give you the gift of tongues." So I did but just as quickly as I asked a huge lump came into my throat. I could hardly speak, like I was choking. I told her. She said, "That's Satan."

"Satan!" I exclaimed, "What's he got to do with this?" Now I really was nervous. Explaining to me that he doesn't want me to have this gift, I got mad. She told me to tell the fear to leave me in the name of Jesus Christ. I did! Suddenly this wonderful exhilarating love language began to flow from my lips! It was glorious! I talked and talked to God! So much to tell Him...so much stored up over the years. By this time everyone had left the church except my friend, who was leaned up against a wall, and me. She asked, "Are you afraid if you leave you'll lose this gift?" Yes I was afraid of that. "Well you can speak in tongues the whole way home in the car!" she responded. And believe me I did!

Summation

The church needs a revival today. There is need for renewal of mission and purpose throughout the church and her individual members. We must recover the dynamic power of the Holy Spirit, which transformed and empowered the early Christians. Many in every major denomination experience speaking in tongues, demonstrating that the baptism in the Holy Spirit is not a denomination or a movement but an experience or encounter with God that brings enduement of spiritual power for intensified on fire ministry to the glory of God.

Listen to Jesus:

"Come, follow me," Jesus said, "and I will make you fishers of men."
(Matthew 4:19, NIV)

"But you shall receive power ... to become My witnesses..."
(Acts 1:8, NKJ)

You have within you a treasure. But we have this treasure in jars of clay to show that this all-surpassing power is from God and not from us.
(2 Corinthians 4:7, NIV)

Prayer for Release of the Holy Spirit

Right now, right where you are just ask God to release His Holy Spirit in you. Ask for all the gifts for He delights to give them to you.

ASK – SURRENDER - BE WILLING – BELIEVE – EXERCISE THE POWER

Chapter 9
WALKING OUT YOUR HEALING IN DAILY VICTORY

What a great healing journey you are on! It's the beginning of a life time of allowing God to heal you at deeper and deeper levels, freeing you from past wounds that have kept you in bondage. Every healing increases your capacity to receive God's love and blessings in order to give out more and more of His love. Now we walk out our healing in daily victory. Walking in daily victory in healing is the process of being sanctified. Spiritual victory comes through a continually renewed relationship with God and your community. Your relationship with God needs to remain new and fresh. Our salvation is assured because of our personal acceptance of Jesus Christ as our Lord and Savior. The challenge of Christian living is to walk in victory daily.

... continue to work out your salvation with fear and trembling.
(Philippians 2:12)

As you have therefore received Christ Jesus the Lord, so walk in Him, rooted and built up in him and established in the faith, as you have been taught, abounding in it with thanksgiving.

(Colossians 2:6-7)

Healing is a Process

Sometimes it seems in healing that we take three steps forward and two back. Healing is a process. Scripture states *I AM the God who heals you* (Exodus 15:26). This simple verse challenges Christians to not trivialize healing by quick answers when healing seems to fail or be a struggle or be delayed. Don't diminish God's divine work because the modern world seeks natural explanations, insisting that human criteria are met in our evaluation of the sustainability of healing. Many Christians, especially in North America, want quick solutions and fast healing. Perseverance, patience, and deeper revelation of healing have been and remain challenges in inner healing.

Healing is a divine work and because this is so, it is difficult to evaluate the sustainability of inner healing as evidenced by transformed lives through Christ reflecting new behavior. It is difficult because we look at healing through human eyes. Healing is cyclic. Think of a spiral. We move forward following a healing and later we are challenged by a temptation or an attack from the enemy. Perhaps we fall back a step or two in our response or lack of response. Suffering happens. In the suffering we are enlarged in heart and encouraged by God to rise up, pick up your mat and walk again. That is the healing process.

At times we do fall and we do fail and God, who is the Healer, calls us back again and again. Remember Peter sinking in the deep water as he walked towards Jesus because his attention was drawn to the rough, scary circumstances all around him instead of being focused on Jesus. He did fall and immediately called out to Jesus who instantly pulled him up. Remember Mary Magdalene, a loving, passionate follower of Christ whom He had delivered from seven demonic spirits, sinking into ungodly sorrow as she searched for a dead Jesus. As Peter was healed and restored so was Mary Magdalene and so are we. Nothing is impossible for God. This brings hope to all who struggle in the healing process.

Someone I prayed with who was struggling with her self-centeredness that continued to plague her stated her goal in healing, "I would also like to be able to regard the person who may be causing me pain, with love, instead of having my awareness focused on myself (Other-centered vs. self-centered)." She had not lost hope in this struggle.

The theologian Karl Barth states *The last word concerning the world of men is not 'Dust thou art and unto dust shalt thou return!' But, because I live, ye shall live also. With this last word in our minds we feel hope and our need stirring within us. The advancing glory of God has already vouchsafed us* (Barth, 1982, p297).

God Initiates and Completes the Process

Scripture clearly declares God is the alpha and the omega and so it is with healing. This realization is not just words but revelation or epiphany. God is faithful and steadfast! And he gives us the power to be faithful and steadfast as we walk out our healings.

Perhaps a better definition of healing has to do with this steadfastness in going on despite difficulty or delay in achieving success. Does healing and living out that healing in spite of setbacks, challenge us all to remain steadfast, devoted to God and who He is, not fearful, and giving Him our undivided attention no matter what? This is a tough challenge and this is the messiness or the loose ends of trying to define healing. One person in the healing process succinctly states this: *I must know I can trust God and not fear that the negative behavior pattern will continue. I can either choose the way of fear or way of love.* Philip Melanchthon writes, *"What the heart desires, the will chooses, and the mind justifies," for healing or destruction* (Valendy, 2017)

Tools for walking out your healing in daily victory: Christian community with accountability and committed relationships, personal scripture study, prayer time, worship both corporate and individual, mission work, and spiritual direction.

The need for Christian community as a support for participants involved in inner healing is crucial for one's success and well-being. Community gives us all the opportunity to share with each other with great transparency both the difficulties of maintaining healing and the joy of Christ even in the struggle. It is astounding and delightful to hear another verbalize your own struggle with life issues like identity and insecurity. It is exciting to share in each other's healing victories. It is in community that we feel such thanksgiving for each other, and the great gifts God has made us for each other. And it is in community we step out together to bring healing to the wounded souls both inside and outside the church.

Martin Luther suffered from severe bouts of depression throughout his life. As I studied his life it became apparent the need for community support and compassion which he didn't have. These bouts of depression in Luther's life which brought him into a devastating aloneness and absolute negation of himself were the ashes from which the heart of his lectures and sermons rose bringing many to hear him. At one point during a time of experiencing terrible night terrors he wrote, *'... I will defy Duke George and all the lawyers and theologians, but when these knaves, the spirits of evil come, the Church must join in the fight...'* (Todd, 1982, p 343). The Church must join together in community in the fight of healing and deliverance of God's people.

If you want to grow in your Christian walk you must have committed relationships with other Christians. We need other Christians who will hold us accountable for progress on our healing journey. Why? Because we are easily deceived. We don't always see ourselves clearly. We need safe places to share. We need others to love us up close and personal with all our warts showing. Our communities must become healing communities where others can look at us and say, *See how they love one another.* We have to spend time with people to build deep relationships.

Personal scripture study is crucial for the development of our inner being. We must take our experiences and match them with the Word of God to trust their authenticity. Our experiences should form God's character in us. His Word is sharper than a two-edged sword. It will separate from your life ungodly things. If you do not know the Word how will you be guided?

> *"All scripture is God-breathed,"* (Timothy 3:16).
>
> *Be washed by the water of the Word,* (Ephesians 5:26).

Pray through these scriptures:

> *May God himself, the God of peace, sanctify you through and through. May your whole spirit, soul and body be kept blameless at the coming of our Lord Jesus Christ. 24 The one who calls you is faithful, and he will do it.*
> **(1 Thessalonians 5:23-24).**
>
> *Let the Word dwell, come to life, in you,* (Colossians 3:16).
>
> *The Word of God changes you,* (Romans 2:4).

Discover Your Gifts

Discover your gifts and allow the Holy Spirit to use them in service to others.

Spend time with God every day. Share your healing with others. Pour out the mercy you've received onto someone else. Pouring out what you have received redeems your pain and increases your capacity to receive more from God into your soul. . Grow in responsibility to your community. Where are you spending your time? Your money? Your talent? Are your resources being spent on reaching unbelievers? God is after your heart.

Remember that the healing process is more cyclic than linear in structure. Healings allow deeper penetration within, newly exposing our natural defects as well as hidden wounds not healed yet. The struggles in maintaining healing demonstrate the struggle for sanctified souls between grace and corruption. And through it all God is with us every day, every minute of our lives! Emmanuel, God with us as we are going through this journey of healing together.

Walking Out Healing Prayer

Thank you, Lord, for Your healing and Your love and compassion for me. You have given me tools and knowledge to continue walking out my healing. Help me to be a good steward daily of these tools.

I present to You my soul and my body as a living sacrifice. Lord, I give You permission to crucify my sinful nature daily in order that I may have Your character built into me. I give You all my anxiety and fears in exchange for Your peace and perfect love. I surrender my soul to You.

Holy Spirit be my teacher. Daily show me the way of truth and love. Teach me how to serve You and others. Teach me how to surrender my plans and instead receive Your plans for my life. Renew my mind and heart. Show me how to be a godly friend. (If married how to be a godly spouse and parent.). Help me to make good heathy decisions about my body. Bring me into deeper relationship with You and teach me how to worship You and pray to You. When I fail, show me Your mercy, Your truth and how much You love me.

Help me to daily walk with You and with Your help, daily walk out my healing in the community of Your Body. Lord help me to love others as You love. Make me an instrument of Your peace and grace, an ambassador of reconciliation for Your glory and honor. Amen.

Thank you dear reader for coming on this pilgrimage journey of healing with me. I pray that the healing God has accomplished and is accomplishing in you sets your hearts afire to desire more and more healing to become His healers. Bless you precious child of God. Bless you mighty warrior. Bless you with His mercy and grace. And bless you with His gift of healing. You are more than you know. The Lord has need of you! You are of great value to God and He will never leave you.

The Lord bless you and keep you; the Lord make his face to shine upon you and be gracious to you; the Lord lift up his countenance upon you and give you peace. (Leviticus 6: 24-26)

WORKS CONSULTED

Alcoholics Anonymous (1988) *The Twelve Steps – A Spiritual Journey.* Curtis, Washington: RPI Publishing, Inc.

Augsburger D. W. (1996) *Helping People Forgive.* Louisville: Westminster John Knox Press.

Barth, K. trans Douglas Horton. (1982) *The Word of God & the Word of Man.* New York: Harper & Bennett, Rita. *Emotionally Free.* North Brunswick: Bridge-Logos Publishers.

Brainy Quotes (2019) *Saint Augustine quotes.* Retrieved 8/8/2019 from https://www.brainyquote.com/quotes/saint_augustine_120609

Beliefnet (2019) *31 Sneaky Lies the Enemy Wants You to Believe.* Retrieved 8/8/2019 from http://www.beliefnet.com/Faiths/Galleries/31-Sneaky-Lies-the-Enemy-Wants-You-to-Believe.aspx?p=19#KHHqi2JKFBcqJkdF.99

Bennett, R. (1998) *Emotionally Free Course: Basic Training.* Christian Renewal Assn.

Bennett, R. (2004) *Emotionally Free Course: Basic Training.* Christian Renewal Assn.

Bennett, R. (1991) *Yielding Will to God and Cleansing Imagination Prayer.* Edmonds, WA: Christian Renewal Association, Inc.

Bosworth, F.F. (2000) *Christ the Healer,* 9th ed. Grand Rapids, MI: Revell

Christian Healing Ministries (2019) Retrieved 8/8/2019 from https://www.christianhealingmin.org/

Coppege, A. (2009) *Portraits of God.* Downers Grove: InterVarsity Press.

Cron, I. M. (2006) *Chasing Francis: A Pilgrim's Tale.* New York: Harper Collins.

Dawn, M (chapter 1 p 10) (2001) *Powers, Weakness, and the Tabernacle of God.* Grand Rapids: Eerdmans.

Eaves, S. (Date Unknown) *The I Am Book.* Sarasota, FL.

Elliot, J. (2013, February 1) Quotes from Jim Elliot from 'Through the Gates of Splendor'. *Agape Mission Church.* Retrieved 8/8/2019 from http://w2.agape-churches.org/?p=63

Elishasmantle.com (2014) *Bitter Roots.* Retrieved 8/8/2019 from http://elishasmantle.freeyellow.com/bitterroot.htm

Frost, J. (2006) *Spiritual Slavery to Spiritual Sonship.* Shippensburg, PA: Destiny Image, Inc.

Greer, S. & Morris, T. (1975) Psychological Attributes of Women Who Develop Breast Cancer. *Journal of Psychosomatic Research*, vol 19, 2, p 147-153. Retrieved 8/8/2019 from http://www.sciencedirect.com/science/article/pii/0022399975900628-

Henry, M. (2010) Commentary on Hebrews 6. *Blue Letter Bible.* 1 Mar. 1996. 2010. 17 Sep 2010.

Ilibagiza, Immaculee. *Left To Tell.* Carlsbad: Hay House, 2006. Print.

Ingram, J, Owen, J, Donehey, M. (2010) *This is Where the Healing Begins.* Essential Music Publishing, Spirit Music Group.

Kammer, Charles L. III, "Healing the Human Community: Grace as Reconciliation." *Word and World* II.4 (1982): 369-378. Print.

Kylstra, C. & Kylstra, B. (2001) *Restoring the Foundations: An Integrated Approach in Healing Ministry,* 2nd ed. Hendersonville, NC: Proclaiming His Word Pub.

Kraft, C. H. (1993) *Deep Wounds, Deep Healing.* Ann Arbor: Vine Books/Servant Pub.

LeMarquand, G. R. (2002). *An Issue of Relevance: A Comparative Study of the Story of the Bleeding Woman* (Mk 5:25-34; Mt 9:20-22; Lk 8: 43-48) *in North Atlantic and African Contexts.* Doctoral Thesis: Wycliffe College and the U of Toronto..

Lewis, C. S. (1942) *The Screwtape Letters.* UK: Geoffrey Bles.

Lewis, Sharon L Gottfried. (2016) *Healing School Level 1 Workbook: A Course in Inner Healing.* Florida: Xulon Press.

Lewis, Sharon L Gottfried. (2012) *Evaluating the Sustainability of Inner Healing as Evidenced by Transformed Lives through Christ, Reflecting New Behavior.* PA: Trinity School for Ministry: Doctoral dissertation.

Linn, M & Linn, D. (1978) *Healing Life's Hurts: Healing of Memories through Five Stages of Forgiveness.* New York: Paulist Press.

Lockman Foundation (1999) *Jesus Saves New Testament.* La Habra, CA.

Manning, B. (1994) *Abba's Child: the Cry of the Heart for Intimate Belonging.* Menasha, WI: NavPress Publishing Group.

MacNutt, F. (1974) *Healing.* U of Notre Dame: Ave Maria Press.

May, G. G. (1988) *Addiction and Grace.* San Francisco: Harper & Row.

McGrath, Al. E. (1999) *The Journey: A Pilgrim in the Lands of the Spirit.* London: Doubleday, 1999.

___(1996 *A Passion for Truth.* Downers Grove: InterVarsity, 1996.

Monroe, P. G. & Schwab, G. M. (2009) God as Healer: a Closer Look at Biblical Images of Inner Healing with Guiding Questions for Counselors. *Journal of Psychology and Christianity* 28.2 (2009): 121-129.

Morse, J. Roback (2001, January 1) The Problem with Living Together. *Focus on the Family*. Retrieved 8/8/2019 from https://www.focusonthefamily.com/marriage/the-problem-with-living-together/

Mumford, N. (2011) *After the Trauma the Battle Begins*. Troy, NY: Troy Book Makers. (chapter 1 p 10)

Nouwen, H. J. M. (2002) *Life of the beloved: and, Our greatest gift*. London: Hodder & Stoughton.

Oden, T. C. (2009) *Classic Christianity: A Systematic Theology*. New York, NY: HarperCollins.

----- (1983) *Pastoral Theology*. San Francisco: Harper & Row.

Packer, J.I. (1993) *Knowing God*. Downers Grove: InterVarsity.

____ (1992) *Rediscovering Holiness*. Ann Arbor: Servant Publications, 1992.

Payne, L. (1986) *Restoring the Christian Soul: Overcoming Barriers to Completion in Christ Through Healing Prayer*. Grand Rapids, MI: Baker Books.

____ (1995) *The Healing Presence: Curing the Soul Through Union with Christ*. Grand Rapids: Baker Books.

Prayer Book and Hymnal: Book of Common Prayer. (1986) New York: Church Pub.

Richardson, D. (2012) *Family Ties that Bind: A Self-Help Guide to Change Through Family of Origin Therapy* USA/Canada: International Self-Counsel Press, Ltd.

Saint Augustine R. C. Church (2019) *Saint Augustine Quotes*. Retrieved 8/8/2019 from https://staugny.org/quotes

Sanford, J. A. (1992) *Ministry Burn Out.* Louisville, KY: Westminster John Knox Press.

Savard, L. (2012) *Breaking the Power of Unmet Needs, Unhealed Hurts, and Unresolved Issues in Your Life,* revised and updated. Gainesville: Bridge-Logos

_____ (1992) Savard, Liberty. *Shattering Your Strongholds.* Gainesville: Bridge-Logos, 1992. Print.

_____ (2002) *The Unsurrendered Soul.* Gainesville, FL: Bridge-Logos.

Smith, E. M. (1999) *Beyond Tolerable Recovery.* Campbellsville: Alathia Pub.

Stapleton, R. C. (1977) *The Experience of Inner Healing.*

Talmud Berakhoth (2010) *Talmud of the Land of Israel Tricate Blessings.* Retrieved 8/8/2019 from http://halakhah.com/yerushalmi_berakhot_tzvee_zahavy_2010.pdf

Thayer, H. (2019) *Greek English Lexicon of the New Testament.* Retrieved 8/8/2019 from http://www.biblesupport.com/e-sword-downloads/file/10618-thayers-unabridged-greek-english-lexicon-of-the-new-testament/

The Bible: *English Standard Version.* Wheaton: Crossway Bibles, 2007. Print.

The Bible: *New American Standard Bible.* Anaheim: Foundation, 1997. Print.

The Bible: *New International Version.* Grand Rapids: Zondervan Bible Pub., 1973. Print.

[The] Chalice (1998)

Todd, J. M. (1982) *Luther: A Life.* New York: Cross Road, 1982.

Tozer, A. W. (2019) A. W. Tozer Quotable Quotes. *Goodreads. com* Retrieved 8/8/2019 from https://www.goodreads.com/quotes/369949-has-it-ever-occurred-to-you-that-one-hundred-pianos

Valendy, J. (2017) *Be the Change.* Retrieved 8/8/2019 from http://www.jasonvalendy.net/blog/2017/4/25/what-the-heart-loves-the-will-chooses-and-the-mind-justifies

Volf, M. (2006) *The End of Memory: Remembering Rightly in a Violent World.* Cambridge, UK: Wm B Eerdmans Publishing Co.

Webster's New Collegiate Dictionary (2014) Miriam Webster, Inc.

CONTACT INFORMATION:

Amazing Love Healing Ministry

Email: info@amazinglovehealing.com

Website: www.amazinglovehealing.com (subscribe to our mailing list)

Amazing Love Healing Ministry is a non-profit, interdenominational and international 501c3 ministry. Thousands have come through our healing conferences, schools of training, and private appointments. We are committed to carrying out God's mandate to us to plant healing houses all over the world for the healing and sending out of His people.

Resources: workbooks on Amazon and our web site:

Healing School Level 1 workbook
Healing School Level 1 workbook Spanish edition
Healing School Level 2 workbook

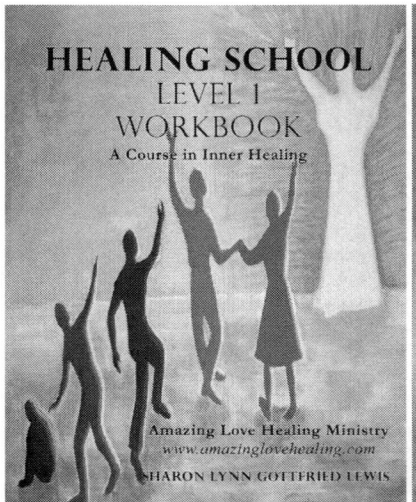

DVD's available for purchase for Amazing Love Healing Ministry teachers. Contact us: info@amazinglovehealing.com

Amazing Love Healing Ministry offers:
    Introduction to Healing

Healing Schools for Training
    Healing Explosion Events
    Prayer Facilitator Training
    Inner Healing Conferences

It is our hope that as a result of reading this book and experiencing inner healing yourself that you will be encouraged to attend one of our healing schools or healing conferences to experience personally greater freedom in Jesus Christ and be further equipped to pray healing prayers with others for their renewal and freedom. You are needed!

Made in the USA
Columbia, SC
21 September 2019